The Book of Guinness Advertising

**The zoo-keeper and his menagerie pose before the main gate of the Guinness Brewery in Dublin.
A painting by John Gilroy for the cover of *Guinness Harp* magazine, January–February 1959.**

The Book of

GUINNESS

ADVERTISING

Brian Sibley

GUINNESS
BOOKS

Dedicated to my
FATHER
who began my interest
in both the business of brewing
and the art of advertising
and
to all those
Artists, Writers, Photographers
and Film-makers
whose
Guinness Advertisements
have given us both so much pleasure

Editor: Beatrice Frei
Design and layout: Lawrence Edwards
First published in 1985
© Brian Sibley and Guinness Superlatives, 1985

Published in Great Britain
by Guinness Superlatives Ltd,
2 Cecil Court, London Road,
Enfield, Middlesex

Typeset in 10/11pt Imprint
by Fakenham Photosetting Ltd,
Fakenham, Norfolk.
Printed and bound in Italy
by Arnoldo Mondadori Editore

British Library Cataloguing in Publication Data
Sibley, Brian
Guinness advertising: The book of
1. Arthur Guinness Son and Co. (Park Royal) –
History   2. Advertising – Great Britain –
Brewing industry – History
I. Title
659.1'96633'0941   HF6161.B5
ISBN 0–85112–400–3

Over the past 55 years, Guinness advertising has provided interest, excitement and even controversy. It is difficult sometimes to accept that the role of advertising is to encourage sales and the commercial aspect is paramount. That so many people have taken pleasure from it – and proudly boast of their association with its creation – places Guinness advertising in a very special category.

The Book of Guinness Advertising is for all of them. In writing this history, Brian Sibley has objectively pieced together an enjoyable narrative which, I am certain, will bring back thoughts of earlier days. I would like to congratulate him for chronicling the Guinness advertising legend.

Just as the famous product is finding new followers throughout the world, Guinness advertising begins a new, as yet unwritten, chapter with the next phase. Its part in the legend will be told another day.

To all of those within Guinness, advertising agencies, artists, photographers and support staff who have worked on the many campaigns, I extend my gratitude. Most of all, I would like to thank the consumers for their continuing appreciation of Guinness.

ERNEST SAUNDERS

Contents

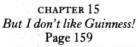

GUINNESS
FOR STRENGTH

A Guinness Book-opener

A preface ought to be thought of rather like a bottle-opener. Not designed as a thing of particular beauty in itself, but a practical device, nevertheless, enabling one to get quickly inside and begin consuming the contents.

Some people, of course, do not read prefaces. They are like a person who would rather smash the neck off a Guinness bottle than open it in the conventional way. By now, they are probably half way through the book, but to those who can contain their thirst a little longer, I would offer a word or two by way of introduction.

What must be understood from the outset, is that this is a highly personal view of Guinness advertising by someone who does not work in brewing and has never worked in advertising. His only qualifications, in fact, are that he drinks Guinness and has great affection for the advertising which first introduced him to it. As a result, this book is primarily intended for other such devotees. Hopefully, however, it will not be without some interest to students and practitioners of advertising.

Research into the public's attitude to Guinness advertising, undertaken in preparing the recent 'Friends of the Guinnless' campaign, showed that people have strongly held opinions on the subject. Some thought it clever, some thought it precious, but all of them had clear, if conflicting, views about Guinness as a result of the advertisements they had seen. Here, for the first time, is the story behind those advertisements – the story of how Guinness advertising came into being and how it has developed over the past fifty-five years.

Piecing together this story has involved a good deal of detective work. Although at the time of my researches, there were no formal Guinness archives, I managed to look at every Guinness poster, press advertisement, TV and cinema commercial. There was, I discovered, enough material to fill not one, but several volumes.

The process of selecting illustrations was, therefore, a difficult one, and I apologise if I have omitted anyone's personal favourite. The process of selection was made harder by the fact that much of the material could not easily be reproduced. For example, a still picture from a film commercial can give, at best, only a dim impression of what may have worked brilliantly on the cinema or TV screen. There were problems also with some of the printed material. Because advertising was, for many years, considered little more than ephemeral, original art-work was often discarded or lost, and printed advertisements were simply pulled from newspapers and magazines and pasted into large scrapbooks. These are known in the advertising industry as 'guard books', but they were guarded for the reference of sales and marketing departments, not for eventual publication in art books.

Consequently, there are some illustrations in this book which clearly show the ravages of time, but in all such cases it was thought preferable for them to be seen in less than perfect condition than not to be seen at all.

In the course of my research, I endeavoured to meet as many as possible of those involved in commissioning and producing Guinness advertising. They gave me much help, which I am pleased to acknowledge here.

Firstly, I am grateful to Ernest Saunders, the chief executive of Guinness, who has given this project his enthusiastic support and encouragement, allowing me the freedom to fully investigate my subject and express my opinions.

Of the people with whom I have discussed Guinness advertising, several were in retirement and might, therefore, not unreasonably have hoped to have said goodbye to all that. They didn't, and I am particularly grateful for their readiness to revive old memories and relive old experiences. They were (in alphabetical order): Tony Anthony – whose own researches into Guinness advertising provided me with much initial information, Eric Beedell, the late Stanley Penn, Ken Tyrrel, George Wigglesworth and Alan Wood.

Not retired, but no longer involved with Guinness, were Mike Constantinidi, Brian Flint, George Harrison and Frank Nolan.

At Guinness Brewery (G.B.) Ltd.: those directly in charge of advertising at Guinness, marketing director Gary Luddington, and general managers Paul McGrane and Ian Vale; also Neda Abrams, Freda Coomber, Pat Corby-Jones, Edward Guinness, Denise Nichols, Joan Weston and Jean Williams.

At Arthur Guinness Son & Co. (Dublin) Ltd.: Brian Brown, Tom Martin, Aiden O'Hanlon (now retired).

At Guinness Overseas Ltd.: John Devonport, Jane Greenwood and Joan Needham.

At J. Walter Thompson Company Ltd.: Jeremy Bullmore, David Holmes, Alec Morrison and Tom Rayfield.

At Allen, Brady and Marsh Ltd.: Peter Bear and Peter Marsh.

Thanks are also due to Trevor Jacobs of Arks Ltd., Greg Jones of McConnell's Advertising Service Ltd., John Bowden of James Haworth, Peter Cooper of CRAM, Alan Brewster, Denis Crutch, Rowland Emett, Dr Selwyn H. Goodacre, John Halas, Mrs Annetta Hoffnung and Paul Jennings. Also Ogilvy & Mather, Richard Williams Animation Ltd., and Walt Disney Productions.

I am indebted to Charles Hennessy and W. H. Allen for kind permission to quote from *Nobody Else is Perfect*; and to the authors of the following works which have given me much valuable information: *Guinness's Brewery in the Irish Economy 1759–1876* by Patrick Lynch and John Vaizey; *Guinness* by Peter Walsh; *The Persuasion Industry* by John Pearson and Graham Turner; and *Ad: An Inside View of Advertising* by Micky Barnes.

In a special category of their own are those people to whom I repeatedly turned for information, advice and encouragement and who never failed me. I am grateful to them not only for their help, but also for their valued friendship. They are John Gilroy, David Hall, Bruce Hobbs, Gwyn Norris, John Trench and Mike Vineall.

My final thanks go to Guinness Superlatives, who commissioned the book; Lawrence Edwards, who is responsible for its attractive design; Beatrice Frei, my hard-working, long-suffering editor and Barbara Edwards, her ever-patient assistant. For whatever pleasures and insights are to be found within the book, the foregoing people are jointly responsible. Any errors, omissions and short-comings are, I am happy to say, my own unaided work.

Brian Sibley
March 1985

GUINNESS
IS GOOD FOR YOU

GIVES YOU STRENGTH

1

YOU KNOW THAT GUINNESS POSTER?

I t's an odd thing, but the public thinks it owns Guinness advertising! You and I – and millions of other people of all ages and from all walks of life – have the most curious proprietorial attitude towards it. And Guinness have encouraged us in this – even allowed us to imagine that we've thought up their advertising ourselves. Such a relationship between an advertiser and its customers is unique.

You know that
GUINNESS Poster?

" D'you mean that one with the bird with the absurdly long beak—what d'you call those things?...Toucan, that's it! With a great yellow beak, and some kind of rhyme underneath—how does it go?... 'If you can say as I can Guinness is good for you'...and then something about 'how grand to be a toucan, just see what toucan do!'...Terrible pun!...Is that the poster you mean?"

" Yes, that's the one. Have you seen it?"

" No, I never look at advertisements ".

Consider, for example, the thousands of verses, jokes and drawings which the public sends Guinness every year in the hope of coming up with the next Guinness advertisement. Consider the nationwide anxiety when the loquacious toucan went missing; or the torrent of helpful telephone calls to the Guinness Brewery at Park Royal erroneously pointing out an unbelievable spelling error on the 'Guinnless isn't good for you' poster.

Quite simply, Guinness advertising has become an institution – like tea and cricket, fish and chips or Gilbert and Sullivan.

There have, of course, been plenty of other well-known, much-loved and long-remembered advertising campaigns, like the Ovaltineys and the Bisto Kids, the Robertson's Golly, the Murraymints Guardsman and the Esso Tiger. So what makes Guinness advertising so special?

Like the man in the 1947 advert (left), there are thousands of people who 'never look at advertisements', but who, nevertheless, have the latest one from Guinness by heart. What is more, people don't just remember one Guinness advertisement, they remember several – if they are true devotees, dozens. There was the ostrich who swallowed the zoo-keeper's Guinness, glass and all; there was the man with sufficient Guinness-given strength to carry a huge iron girder single-handed; there were all those 'terrible puns', like 'Tall, dark and havesome' or 'Open and say aaah!'; there was that highly intelligent, talking toucan, who knew which football team won the F.A. Cup in 1958; and, more recently, the Friends of the Guinnless with their therapy sessions to help those poor unfortunates who have forgotten to have a Guinness.

But Guinness advertising is not just a subject for fond remembrance; nowadays, it is also a subject for the specialist collector. Everything – from original artwork to old Guinness labels – has a price and a buyer. Pottery toucans are to be found cohabiting antique-shop windows with Staffordshire dogs, and Guinness booklets illustrated by such distinguished artists as Rex Whistler and Edward Ardizzone are now listed among rare first editions in the best booksellers' catalogues. While dealers in advertising ephemera are cashing in on late Guinness joys, Guinness themselves are busily manufacturing tomorrow's collectables: golden harp-shaped pendants; bath-towels, tea-towels, T-shirts, sweaters, track-suits and dressing-gowns; and a cuddly toucan-toy named Arthur. All of which is perfectly natural for Guinness, who, for over two hundred years, have made a habit of turning up anywhere and everywhere.

All Guinness advertising has done is to provide a focal point for people's interest in, and affection for, Guinness itself. That curious-

Left: '**My Goodness – My Guinness!**' **War-time advertisement for service magazines by H. M. Bateman (1943).**
Below right: **Press advertisement by Mel Calman (1970).**
Below left: **Ceramic Guinness characters (1955/56).**

I've just remembered I can't do this...

calman

Give him a Guinness!

14

looking drink with a curious-sounding name.

In the United Kingdom, Guinness advertising has been handled by only four agencies during the past fifty-seven years: S. H. Benson, J. Walter Thompson, Allen, Brady & Marsh and, currently Ogilvy and Mather. Few advertisers, however, can boast of so distinguished a roll call of creative talent as that which has worked on Guinness advertising. Included have been writers such as Dorothy L. Sayers, Paul Jennings and A. P. Herbert; graphic designers like Tom Eckersley and Abram Games; artists and illustrators as diverse as Ronald Searle, John Nash, Quentin Blake, Antony Groves-Raines, Erté, Victoria– and, of course, John Gilroy; and, at some time or other, virtually every major British cartoonist, including Bateman, Fougasse, Emett, Hoffnung, Calman, and Giles.

With such multifarious talent, it is not surprising to find that Guinness has appeared in many different settings, and with a variety of supporting players. Nevertheless, with its fulsome body and beautiful head, Guinness has always been the hero of its own advertising. In fact, Guinness is a star. A star who has rarely shared top-billing with other personalities. There was, however, one occasion, in 1952, when Guinness entered into a fleeting collaboration with another performer of the same name, who was currently starring in the film, *The Card*. But it didn't last.

It is tempting to talk about Guinness advertising as if it were a generic term, describing a particular type or style of advertising. But this is not the case. In its form, content and approach, Guinness advertising has been as varied as the communications media it has employed. That variety is a result of a number of important economic and social factors, not least of which has been the radical change in public attitudes towards marketing which has taken place during the past half-century.

In a moment of excessive cynicism, that Cassandra of the twentieth century, George Orwell, described advertising as 'the rattling of a stick inside a swill bucket'. Today, he would probably be surprised at both the control that society has imposed on advertisers, and the sophistication which they have adopted in response.

Guinness has always been among the leaders in the development of the craft of advertising and, from the outset, they have been particularly conscious of their public responsibilities as an advertiser. No other alcoholic beverage has acquired the universal goodwill possessed by Guinness.

When Guinness first began advertising in 1928, there had been very little study in the field of market-research, and the critical analysis of what came to be called 'the persuasion industry' had yet to take place. In launching that first campaign, however, Guinness decreed that its advertisements 'should at all times be done extremely well and in good taste'.

S. H. Benson Ltd., the advertising agency charged with carrying out that edict, began with a refreshing directness – an appetising pint of what is affectionately called 'the black stuff' and the simple slogan: 'GUINNESS is good for you.'

A few years, some money and a lot of imagination later, Bensons began mixing their Guinness with a dash or two of levity and a jigger of whimsy. The resultant brew proved bubblier than the best Bolinger. It was the beginning of twenty years of fun and frolics with John Gilroy's charming menagerie of Guinness-guzzling animals; and twenty years of the most outrageous puns and parodies.

Among the authors whose work was reworked in the cause of promoting Guinness were Lewis Carroll, Thomas Hood, Edward Lear and W. S. Gilbert. Nothing – or, at least, very little – was sacred; not Chaucer, Longfellow, Wordsworth or Keats.

Advertisement produced for the premiere programme of the 1952 film *The Card*, starring Alec Guinness, and subsequently used as a show-card for off-licence windows during the film's release. Sir Alec's features were also used to decorate drip-mats for public houses!

As Stanley Penn, one of Benson's copywriters, has remarked: 'Guinness always enjoyed their advertising. They liked their advertising to be liked.' And so it was.

When Bensons took charge of its public image, Guinness was already a household name. What Bensons gave that name was character and personality; they made it a friend rather than just a mere acquaintance. And, as with the best of good companions, nobody minded the fact that Guinness was forever putting in an appearance – on hoardings and bus sides; in newspapers and magazines; in zoo guides and theatre programmes; in souvenir brochures for cricket matches, boxing tournaments, gymkhanas, regattas and flower shows.

Sometimes, Guinness-selling necessitated the use of a mellifluent lyricism – 'How many thousands of tiny globes make up the fairy fabric of the Guinness head, as delicate as the dew, as fine as silk, as smooth as swansdown?'. On other occasions, a rather more prosaic approach was favoured – 'Guinness is of particular value in treating constipation'. Guinness soon became, and has since remained, all things to all men.

And this, more or less, is how things went on for thirty years or so; helping to keep up public morale during the Second World War, and unreservedly joining in the post-war mood of euphoria that was symbolised by the Festival of Britain and the Coronation of Queen Elizabeth II.

By the mid-fifties, Guinness advertising included not only posters and press advertisements, but also their filmic equivalents for the cinema and the media's new child – commercial television.

The frivolities of the fifties ended with a bicentennial celebration of Guinness brewing, and the introduction of Guinness advertising in the Republic of Ireland, where Guinness had hitherto had so large a share of the beer market as to make advertising superfluous.

Then came the sixties, and the emergence of the cult of youth. Increasingly, the media turned their spotlight on the young with their miniskirts and Beatlemania. It was an age of change, of old orders giving way to new. Sputniks, dogs and, eventually, men went into orbit around the Earth; while, down below, the young generation outraged the Establishment with its self-conscious interest in pop, pot and satire, mysticism and free love.

In a more serious vein, the sixties saw an increasing awareness among advertisers of the importance of market-research. Guinness were among those who, for the first time,

One of John Gilroy's highly popular animal posters (1956).

Off with its Head !
cried the Queen

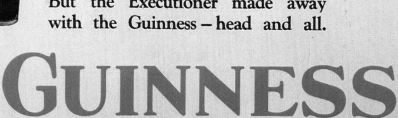

'Nonsense!' cried Alice, 'Guinness keeps its head!'

'Yes,' murmured the King. 'This characteristic creamy foam appears like magic and lingers like–like–

'The grin of the Cheshire Cat,' said Alice.

'Come and play croquet,' roared the Queen. 'Guinness builds muscle for sport .... Guinness keeps its Head!'

But the Executioner made away with the Guinness–head and all.

GUINNESS
KEEPS ITS HEAD

A pastiche of an episode from Lewis Carroll's *Alice's Adventures in Wonderland*, designed by John Gilroy for a London Underground poster in 1930.

When Hebe *was difplaced by* Ganymede
To Earth fhe ftraight repair'd with frantick Speed,
Whither arriving, fhe was much furprifed
To find that daedal Mortals had devifed
For their Refrefhment, an Elyfian Brew
Surpaffing far the Nectar that fhe knew.
So Skyward the celeftial Bar-maid foar'd
Where Gods and Goddeffes with one- Accord,
Who tafted of this Lickour's Strength and Flavour,
Received her back into her wonted Favour.
With Chaunts of Praife and Thanks Olympus *rings*
For all the Health and Vigour GUINNESS *brings.*

Left: **Press advertisement featuring an 'Ode on a Grecian Urn' by John Trench (1952).**
Right: **Theatre programme advertisement (1963).**
Below: **One of the many Guinness advertisements to use a sporting theme, on this occasion the 1948 London Olympic Games.**

The house lights up.
In the interval

GUINNESS
is served in the bar

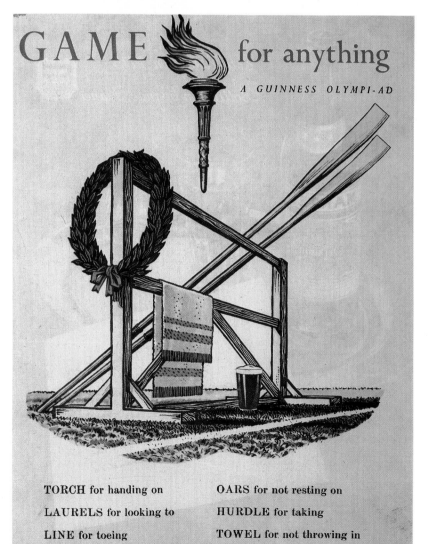

GAME for anything

A GUINNESS OLYMPI-AD

TORCH for handing on   OARS for not resting on

LAURELS for looking to   HURDLE for taking

LINE for toeing   TOWEL for not throwing in

GUINNESS for Strength

began seriously to analyse the consumption, and consumers, of their products. Their findings brought about a dramatic change in their approach to advertising. The whimsical atmosphere of a literary lunch at the zoo was abandoned in favour of a more 'serious' attitude. Sea lions, ostriches and the denizens of Wonderland made way for the first nationally-used picture of a Real Guinness Drinker. The days of purely intuitive advertising, when the inspired invention of Oxbridge copy-writers held sway, were finally at an end.

In 1969, Guinness decided that they needed to take a fresh look at their advertising strategy, and made the surprising decision to end their forty-year association with Bensons. In Ireland, the advertising account passed to Arks of Dublin, and, in the United Kingdom, to J. Walter Thompson Limited.

The Thompson agency added style and sophistication to Guinness advertising with a memorable series of highly entertaining television commercials, some wickedly clever poster slogans and a fashionable campaign aimed at women drinkers. They also brought the toucan out of retirement and put it to work promoting take-home sales.

By this time, however, Guinness had come under serious pressure from a change in beer-marketing in this country. Guinness, once the only nationally advertised beer, was being increasingly challenged by other brewers. The problem was not made any easier by the fact that Guinness – who have never owned public houses of their own – were dependent on the very brewers with whom they were competing, to sell Guinness alongside their own advertised brews. And, to make matters even worse, there was a marked trend

Above: **Scene from an animated cinema commercial featuring a diminutive conductor at the Albert Hall who, thanks to Guinness, has the strength to support his entire choir. (Richard Williams Animation Ltd., 1960).**
Left: **A stylish advertisement for women's magazines – and the gentlemen that read them! (1976).**
Far left: **One of the posters from the 'Give him a Guinness' campaign that marked the passing of the Guinness advertising account from S. H. Benson to J. Walter Thompson (1970).**

Above: **Poster (1971).**
Below: **Trade advertisement heralding the return of the toucan (1979).**

amongst young drinkers towards lagers and light beers instead of bitters and stouts.

Despite the introduction of draught Guinness, the brewery found themselves in a curious position – they had some of the best-loved advertising in the history of the business, and a product with falling sales figures. To many, it seemed that the Company now had three products on the market: Guinness bottled, Guinness draught and Guinness advertising!

One poster claimed 'Our name is on the tip of your tongue', but while the name may have been, the drink, unfortunately, was not. An earlier poster which had announced '7 million every day and still going down', was proving painfully prophetic.

Critics suggested that Guinness had acquired an image that was somewhat exclusive and rather precious. There were even those who felt that Guinness's adored advertising heritage had become less of a milestone and more of a millstone.

As a result of management changes in 1981, it was decided that Guinness should once again look for a new agency to handle its advertising. Surrounded by a storm of publicity, the country's premier account passed from J. Walter Thompson to Allen, Brady & Marsh, who had already been handling the Guinness Harp Lager account for two years.

Following one of the most detailed market-research surveys ever conducted, ABM launched the Friends of the Guinnless campaign.

Starting at 7.45 pm on 9th November, the star of the new Guinness take-home campaign will be making a big impression on the nation's screens.
Make sure you're ready. Make room for Guinness.

MAKE ROOM FOR GUINNESS.

The world and his wife enjoy GUINNESS

Above: **Irish poster (1961).**
Opposite: **Advertisement produced for quality magazines like** *The Tatler*, **featuring art-work by Antony Groves-Raines (1947).**

Below: **A poster marking the arrival of the Guinnless (1983).**

Just as the first Guinness slogan ever written had been simple and unequivocal – GUINNESS is good for you – the message devised for the eighties was just as direct and forceful – GUINNLESS *isn't* good for you.

This book celebrates the five-and-a-half decades of diverse and imaginative marketing that separates those two slogans, and provides a context in which to view the new Guinness advertising from Ogilvy and Mather.

It has been said that Guinness the drink is 'the result of an infinite capacity for taking pains'; the same could well be said of Guinness advertising. Whether based on inspired guesswork or thoroughly-researched statistics, whether aimed at providing a compelling advertisement or an entertaining *divertissement*, quality has always been pre-eminent.

In addition to selling millions of barrels, bottles and cans of beer, and amusing the public at large, Guinness advertising has coin-cidentally reflected British social history – the values and ideals, the wit and humour and the popular art of a nation. And in its natal land across the Irish Sea, and in almost every corner of the world, Guinness advertising has adapted its message to the culture of a hundred different market-places.

It is this story which will be told in these pages.

It is a story which begins two hundred and sixty years ago, in 1725 . . .

GUINNLESS isn't good for you

He didn't discover Guinness until he was 34;
how old were you?

Above left: **Richard Guinness, father of Arthur Guinness, born c 1690 and known to have been alive in 1766.**
Above right: **Arthur Guinness (1725–1803).**
Left: **Eire postage stamp commemorating Arthur Guinness, issued in 1959.**
Far left: **Press advertisement by Geoff Dunbar (1976).**

2

THIRST PERSON SINGULAR

No doubt Richard Guinness and his wife, Elizabeth, were delighted by the arrival, in 1725, of their first son. They probably hoped he would grow up to be a respected member of the community, perhaps even hold some official post like his father, who was Land Steward to the Most Reverend Arthur Price, Archbishop of Cashel. In their wildest dreams, however, they could not have expected him to make the family name known throughout the whole world.

The baby was christened Arthur, after Archbishop Price, who became the boy's godfather. Clearly, the prelate had great affection for the Guinnesses since, when he died twenty-seven years later, he left in his will the generous sum of one hundred pounds to both Arthur and his father.

One of the duties of Richard Guinness in working for the archbishop had been to supervise the brewing of beer for workers on the estate, and, when Arthur grew up, he followed in his father's footsteps and took up brewing as his career. By the time he was thirty-one, he had a small brewery in Leixlip, County Dublin. We do not know what kind of beer he brewed then, but it was probably the brown beer most commonly consumed at the time. It was brewed with highly coloured malt and, unlike ale, had hops added to it. Many people

A mid-eighteenth-century brewery (from an engraving).

thought this an inferior brew, and a popular ballad of 1725 spoke unflatteringly of Dublin's beer:

> This beer is sour, thin, musty, thick and stale,
> And worse than anything except the ale.

Arthur's beer, one likes to think, was somewhat better.

Evidently, he was a young man of courage and determination, for, in 1759, he decided to hand over the Leixlip brewery to his brother, Richard, and seek his fortune in Dublin. On the face of it, this decision appeared rather reckless since the Dublin brewing business was in a bad way and, in the years following, would sink lower, until, in 1773, a Committee of the Irish House of Commons found that the beer revenue had fallen by £51 000 a year 'not owing to any temporary accident, but to a gradual decay in the trade'. This decay was in no small measure due to the fact that the excise laws favoured imported beers over those indigenously produced.

Nevertheless, Arthur Guinness took over a small, ill-equipped brewery at St James's Gate. It consisted of a copper, a kieve, a mill, two malthouses, stabling for twelve horses and a loft to hold 200 tons of hay. The lease, which he signed, was for 9000 years at an annual rent of £45. On 'swearing day', 1 December 1759, Arthur Guinness entered his signature for the first time in the Minute Book of the Brewers and Maltsters Corporation.

The authoritative tone of the 1976 advertisement (opposite), which claimed Arthur discovered Guinness when he was thirty-four, is actually little more than supposition since there is no precise information as to when Arthur began to brew a beer similar to what we now call Guinness. The earliest records date from 1796, by which time he was brewing porter.

Porter, it is generally accepted, was devised in London in 1722 by a man called Harwood. At the beginning of the eighteenth century, Londoners were drinking a number of very strong beers, described as 'stout', with such colourful names as Pharaoh, Huff-cup and the ominous-sounding Knockdown.

The retail price of these 'stouts' was twice that of ordinary beer, and many drinkers took to a mix of ale, beer and, sometimes, a third type of drink, called Twopenny. Half-and-half was a quart mix of beer and ale; Two-thirds or Three-threads had Twopenny added. Harwood, who had a brewery in Shoreditch in London's East End, produced a beer that combined the elements of the Three-thread mix. He called it Entire or Entire-butt since it was drawn from one butt or cask. It came, eventually, to be known as Porter because the majority of its drinkers were the porters of London's street markets.

By 1796, Arthur Guinness was brewing porter and a weaker beer (with less malt and hops and more water), which he called ale. The latter, which probably resulted from a rise in costs of raw materials during the Napoleonic Wars, was not popular and, after 1799, Arthur stuck to brewing porter. The Guinness porter came in two strengths: the weaker, for immediate consumption in Dublin, was called Town Porter; the stronger, for export to England and abroad, was Superior or, later, Extra Superior Porter.

By this time, Arthur Guinness was a well-established figure in Dublin Society. In 1761, he had married Dublin heiress, Olivia Whitmore, and, two years later, bought a country house at Beaumont, County Dublin. He was a Governor of the Meath Hospital and Master of the Corporation of Brewers. After twenty-five years in the business, he became brewer to Dublin Castle.

For all his respectability, Arthur was first and foremost a sharp man of business, who would go to almost any length to protect his brewery. For example, along with two hundred or so other Irish brewers, Arthur was dependent on having a suitable water supply, which, in his day, was provided by the Dodder/Poodle water course, which fed the city cistern at St James's Gate. As part of the original lease, Arthur was entitled to water 'free of tax or pipe money'.

However, in 1773, an investigating Committee of the Corporation accused Arthur of having increased the size of his water pipes and breached the wall of the water course to draw off large quantities of additional water. Payment was demanded of Arthur, who refused, saying that, if necessary, he would defend his water supply 'by force of arms'. When the city's Sheriff arrived with a body of men, they encountered Arthur's employees and the Master Brewer himself, who seized a pickaxe and declared 'with very much improper language, that they should not proceed' and that if they decided to fill up the water course from end to end, he would immediately reopen it.

Arthur Guinness fathered twenty-one children, of whom ten survived, and, at the time of his death in Dublin in 1803, he had a personal estate valued at around £23 000.

His first son, Hosea, being in Holy Orders, Arthur Guinness was succeeded by his three younger sons, the most dominant of whom was Arthur Guinness the Second, who was thirty-five years old when his father died. Like his father, he became a pillar of Dublin Society; among other things, he was President of the Chamber of Commerce and Governor of the Bank of Ireland. When, in 1821, George IV made a State Visit to Ireland, he was received by Arthur Guinness, so beginning the long and developing social relationship between the Guinnesses and the Royal Family.

In common with many others, Arthur Guinness the Second had business problems due to the post-war recession. By 1824, sales had plummeted to what they had been at the beginning of the century. It was a desperate time, but Arthur Guinness – a man cast in his father's mould – was adamant that recovery was possible. He simply determined to brew the best stout available, and, in 1821, laid down precise instructions for the brewing of 'Extra Superior Porter', which he intended as a stronger beer, using a higher hop rate to ensure its characteristics of 'great stability, softness, mildness and vinosity'.

Extra Superior was an important development. In 1820–21, 1200 barrels of it were brewed, which was 4% of Guinness's total output. Eight years later, Extra Superior represented 28% of the trade and, by 1840, 82%. Arthur Guinness the Second had made the Guinness Brewery the largest in Ireland, and his beer was already being shipped into Britain, first through Bristol, and then through Liverpool.

Before his death in 1855, at the age of eighty-seven, Arthur was joined by his third son, Benjamin Lee Guinness, who succeeded his father and managed to treble the family fortunes. Benjamin became Lord Mayor of Dublin in 1851, and later represented the city as Member of Parliament. Like his father and grandfather, he gave liberally to charitable works, including a sum of £150 000 with which he restored St Patrick's Cathedral, to his own designs, in 1865.

Guinness productivity increased, by 1860, to 125 000 barrels, a figure that rose in the next fifty years to almost two million barrels. Nevertheless, there were some setbacks, chiefly caused by the Great Famine of 1840–45, and, rather surprisingly, from the preaching of a highly successful temperance minister, called Father Matthew.

In 1862 the Guinness Trade Mark label appeared, featuring the O'Neil Harp and the famous Guinness signature.

Benjamin Guinness died in 1868 and what was, by that time, the largest brewery in the world, passed to two of his sons, Arthur Edward and Edward Cecil, the latter of whom had joined the Brewery at the age of fifteen. Within eight years, Arthur, who did not share his brother's interest or expertise, sold out his share (for one million pounds) to Edward, who became sole proprietor. Edward Guinness, a gifted man and an excellent manager of brewery affairs, applied his family's philanthropic reputation to the provision of remarkably advanced social service facilities for his employees. Edward Guinness was also responsible for the Brewery's expansion, building a new brewhouse in 1878, and a new malt store in 1886.

Top to bottom:
Arthur Guinness II (1768–1855).
Benjamin Lee Guinness (1798–1868).
Printers' proof of the first Guinness trade mark label (1862).

Left: **Main entrance to the Guinness Brewery on St James's Street, Dublin,** *c* **1840. The nineteenth-century artist who drew this picture enlarged the late Georgian gateway to a preposterous scale in order to show the brewery within.**
Below left: **A rather more realistic view of the front gate from a photograph,** *c* **1920.**
Below: **Edward Cecil Guinness, First Earl of Iveagh (1847–1927), from a caricature by 'Spy' in** *Vanity Fair* **(1891).**

Benjamin Guinness, Lord Iveagh III (b. 1937).

In the same year Guinness became a public company, raising £6 000 000 for 49% of the equity when it was floated on the London Stock Exchange.

Both Edward and Arthur Guinness, as Lords Ardilaun and Iveagh, were generous benefactors of their city, endowing Dublin with St Stephen's Green, St Patrick's Park, the Iveagh Market and many gifts to Trinity College and the Dublin hospitals.

When Edward Guinness died in 1927, he was succeeded by Rupert Guinness, who ran the company until his retirement in 1962, at the age of eighty-eight. During his chairmanship, he made many contributions to agricultural research and saw an international expansion, beginning with the first overseas Guinness Brewery at Park Royal, London, in 1936.

His son, Arthur Onslow Edward Guinness was killed in action in 1945 and the succession passed to his grandson, Benjamin, Viscount Elveden. The sixth direct descendant from the first Arthur Guinness, Benjamin is the present Earl of Iveagh and chairman of Guinness.

A quarter of a millennium of Guinnesses.

Guinness: the name of a family with a long and celebrated history.

Guinness: the name of a beer that has come to be regarded as a supreme brew among brews.

Guinness: the name of a product which has been more imaginatively, elegantly and persuasively advertised than any other.

PORTER.

"Convivial Curs."

Above left: **Illustration by 'Phiz' for** *The Pickwick Papers* **by Charles Dickens (1837) showing Sam and Tony Weller and a contemporary show-card for 'GUINES'S DUBLIN STOUT'. First used in an advertisement for Guinness in 1929.**
Above right: **Illustration, entitled 'Porter – Health, Peace and Prosperity', from** *The Gentleman's Magazine* **(1794).**
Left: **Illustration from** *My Book of Curs* **by R. R. Scanlan (1840).**

3
ITS OWN ADVERTISEMENT

The trouble with advertising is that it is a very expensive business – unless, that is, you can get people to promote your product simply for the love of it, which is what happened with Guinness. Long before the Brewery ever thought of advertising – in fact, long before advertising as we now know it even existed – writers and artists were merrily promoting Guinness for no charge whatsoever.

When, eventually, Guinness did begin advertising, they were quick to capitalise on this legacy of complimentary copy-writing, and some of the resulting advertisements form the illustrations to this chapter.

'The comliest of black malts,' wrote George Saintsbury in *Notes on a Cellar Book*, 'is, of course, that noble liquor called of Guinness.' So comely and so noble that a pair of lips scarcely savoured it before they were commending it.

An engraving of a porter, in *The Gentleman's Magazine* of 1794, was one of the first unpaid advertisements for Guinness.

The caption appended to this picture – 'Health, Peace and Prosperity' – would, sadly, have difficulty in passing today's rigorous advertising standards. Somebody, however, who might well have attested to its truthfulness is a character in Charles Dickens's *Sketches by Boz*, published in 1836.

In the sketch of 'The Boarding House', a new resident comes to live in Mrs Tibbs's house in Great Coram Street. She is Mrs Bloss, a fat, red-faced lady 'in a bonnet the colour of the interior of a damson pie with a regular conservatory of artificial flowers'. Her possessions arrive at her new accommodation, as Dickens puts it 'by instalments' the first of which is 'a large hamper of Guinness's stout, and an umbrella'. Clearly, Mrs Bloss is a lady with excellent priorities! Indeed, she needs little excuse to down a glass of stout, as can be seen from her response to the revelation that her landlady is married: ' "Married!" said Mrs Bloss, taking a draught of Guinness – "married! Unpossible!" '

A pictorial reference to Guinness appears in Dickens's next book, *The Pickwick Papers* (1837). An illustration by 'Phiz' (Hablot K. Browne) shows Sam and Tony Weller in the Blue Boar, in 'Leaden'all Markit', where Sam is reading his father a valentine he has just composed. A card on the mantelpiece behind the elder Mr Weller advertises GUINES'S DUBLIN STOUT.

This illustration is probably one of the earliest examples of how not to spell GUINNESS! Another good way of not spelling it is shown in a drawing by R. R. Scanlan for *My Book of Curs* (opposite).

In 1837, the same year that Guinness (however it was spelt) was being quaffed at the Blue Boar in Leadenhall Market, it was also being enjoyed in the rather more sedate surroundings of the Carlton Club – on one memorable evening, during his first Parliament, by the young Benjamin Disraeli. In a letter to his sister Sarah, on 21 November 1837, Disraeli recorded both his party's political triumph and the Guinness supper which followed.

It is not known whether Queen Victoria herself ever tasted the delights of Guinness, but the death of her beloved Albert in 1861 was responsible for the introduction of what is still regarded as a prince among drinks – Black Velvet. At the time, the whole of London was in mourning for the Consort, and the bar steward at Brooks's Club in St James's Street decided that the champagne should also go into mourning – to achieve this, he simply mixed it with Guinness! When it was first called Black Velvet, or who gave it that elegant name, is not known; for many years it was called 'Bismarck' after the Iron Chancellor who may have sampled the drink when he visited England in 1862. A cartoon by Linley Sambourne appeared in *Punch* on 13 September 1884, showing Bismarck contemplating

Right: A letter written by Benjamin Disraeli to his sister, Sarah, on 21 November 1837: ['So, after all, there was a division on the Address in Queen Victoria's first Parliament] 509 to 20. The division took an hour. I then left the house at ten o'clock, none of us scarcely having dined. The tumult and excitement unprecedented. I dined or rather supped at the Carlton with a large party of the flower of our side off oysters, Guinness, and broiled bones, and got to bed at ½ past 12. Thus ended the most remarkable day hitherto of my life.' This facsimile was frequently used in advertisements from 1929.

THE VERY "OLD SOLDIER."

The Ever-busy B. (considering). "WHY NOT ANOTHER CONFERENCE? GOOD! CONDUCTED THIS TIME IN OUR OWN BEAUTIFUL TONGUE. BETTER!! AND AS JOHN BULL IS TOO INTERESTED IN HIS DOMESTIC AFFAIRS TO THINK OF ANYTHING ELSE—HEM!—WE SHALL HAVE TO MEET WITHOUT HIM! BEST!!!"

Linley Sambourne cartoon
in *Punch*, 13 September 1884,
showing Bismarck to have
had a taste for Guinness and
champagne.

a conference (without a British presence) to discuss Egyptian finances. On his desk stand a bottle of Guinness and a bottle of bubbly.

If only Guinness advertising had been underway, Sambourne could have simply captioned his cartoon: 'Things look Brighter after a Guinness.'

Over the years, Guinness copywriters have used some outrageous rhymes, but none more contorted than that which appears in one of Richard Barham's *Ingoldsby Legends* of 1842 (a work later parodied as *The Guinness Legends*). In 'A Legend of Spain', Barham describes the Court of King Ferdinand:

> ...While many a suitor
> And gay coadjutor
> In the eating-and-drinking line, scorns to be neuter;
> One, being perhaps just return'd with his tutor
> From travel in England, is tempting his '*future*'
> With a luxury neat as imported, 'The Pewter'
> And charming the dear Violantes and Iñeses
> With a three-corner'd Sandwich, and a soupçon of 'Guinness's'.

Barham was grammatically correct in his spelling of 'Guinness's', as is amusingly borne out by *The Comic English Grammar* of 1840:

> The Possessive Case is distinguished by an apostrophe, with the letter *s* subjoined to it: as, 'My soul's idol!' – 'A pudding's end' ... When the singular terminates in *ss*, the letter *s* is sometimes dispensed with: as 'For goodness' sake!' Nevertheless, we have no objection to 'Guinness's' Stout.

It is interesting to observe the happy conjunction of the name of Guinness with the phrase 'For goodness' sake!' almost a hundred years before the same notion occurred to Guinness themselves.

Someone who, like our comic grammarian, had no objection to Guinness's Stout was a character in W. M. Thackeray's *Burlesques*:

> 'Here goes,' said Tom Delancey, and sung the following lyric of his own composition:–
> 'Dear Jack, this white mug that with Guinness I fill,
> And drink to the health of sweet Nan of the Hill...'

One splendid little paean which Guinness appear to have overlooked (or perhaps rejected since it mentions rival beers) was composed by that great comic versifier, C. S. Calverley:

> O Beer! O Hodgson, Guinness, Allsopp, Bass!
> Names that should be on every infant's tongue!

Although Guinness were to later claim that their name was on the tip of our tongues, it is doubtful if they expected that to apply to quite so youthful a category of drinkers as Calverley envisaged.

In addition to referring to Guinness in their public writings, many men and women of letters have privately recorded their fondness for the drink.

Two of the most famous testimonials were supplied by Jane Welsh Carlyle, the wife of the Scottish writer Thomas Carlyle, and by Robert Louis Stevenson.

In a letter dated 19 February 1893, written aboard the s.s. *Mariposa*, Stevenson wrote: 'Fanny ate a whole fowl for breakfast, to say nothing of a tower of hot cakes. Belle and I floored another hen betwixt the pair of us, and I shall be no sooner done with the present amanuensing racket than I shall put myself outside a pint of Guinness. If you think this looks like dying of consumption in Apia I can only say I differ from you.'

Stevenson wasn't the only, or indeed the first, person to enjoy Guinness overseas. One of the earliest accounts of its foreign travels is to be found in the diary of a Cavalry Officer who was wounded while fighting at the Battle of Waterloo in 1815.

During the Crimean War of 1854–56, the *Ashford & Alfred News* reported that 'a vessel has been chartered to convey 500 hogsheads of Messrs Guinness's porter to Constantinople direct'.

Several thousand miles from Constantinople, in the tropical jungles of Brazil, the naturalist T. W. Hinchliff wrote of the extraordinary restorative qualities of Guinness: 'It was almost too hot for midday rambles, especially as we continued to wear ordinary English shooting clothes. On reaching a stream I was compelled to sit with my feet in the water and bathe my head with a wet handkerchief. While I was in this position a purple fresh-water crab walked across my toes, and the largest blue butterfly that I had ever seen was fluttering in the sunshine. On getting back to our quarters, I found that the ferns in the vasculum had dried like hay; my clothes were dripping, and we were both very glad to apply the best remedy that I know for over-exertion in a hot climate. It consists of simply drinking a bottle of Guinness before doing anything else. The cure is instantaneous.'

In fact, Guinness could be relied upon to turn up just about anywhere – whether at the equator or the pole someone was always testifying to the benefits of a Guinness.

What all these testimonials demonstrate is

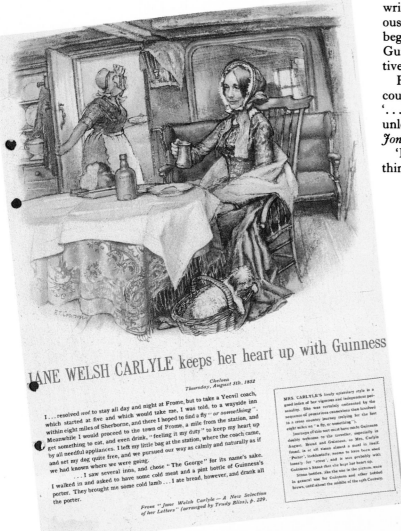

JANE WELSH CARLYLE keeps her heart up with Guinness

Chelsea
Thursday, August 5th, 1852

I ... resolved *not* to stay all day and night at Frome, but to take a Yeovil coach, which started at five and which would take me, I was told, to a wayside inn within eight miles of Sherborne, and there I hoped to find a fly "*or something*". Meanwhile I would proceed to the town of Frome, a mile from the station, and get something to eat, and even drink, "feeling it my duty" to keep my heart up by all needful appliances. I left my little bag at the station, where the coach came, and set my dog quite free, and we pursued our way as calmly and naturally as if we had known where we were going.

... I saw several inns, and chose "The George" for its name's sake. I walked in and asked to have some cold meat and a pint bottle of Guinness's porter. They brought me some cold lamb ... I ate bread, however, and drank all the porter.

From "Jane Welsh Carlyle — A New Selection of her Letters" (arranged by Trudy Bliss), p. 229.

MRS. CARLYLE'S lively epistolary style is a good index of her vigorous and independent personality. She was certainly undaunted by the sequence of precarious connexions then involved in a cross country journey (relying for the last eight miles of "a fly, or something").

Journeys of this sort must have made Guinness doubly welcome to the traveller, especially in August. Bread and Guinness, as Mrs. Carlyle found, is at all times almost a meal in itself. 'Porter', incidentally, seems to have been used loosely for 'stout', and it was probably with Guinness's Stout that she kept her heart up.

Stone bottles, like the one in the picture, were in general use for Guinness and other bottled brews, until about the middle of the 19th Century.

writer O. Henry recalled being served a curious meal in which the courses came in threes beginning with 'guinea-fowls, guinea-pigs and Guinness's stout'. A somewhat bizarre alternative to the more usual oysters and Guinness.

Francis Brett Young refers to Guinness on a couple of occasions, in *Jim Redlake* (1930) – '... Don't mention bottled stuff, Mr Redlake, unless it be Guinness' – and in *My Brother Jonathan* (1928):

'I thought you'd be better for a bite of something,' said Joseph. 'And I took the liberty of

Left: **Magazine advertisement featuring the testimonial of Jane Welsh Carlyle, illustrated by R. T. Cowern (1955).**
Below: **A recommendation from a soldier who fought at the Battle of Waterloo, with a contemporary caricature of the Duke of Wellington. First used as a Guinness advertisement in 1933.**

that for hundreds of years people have viewed Guinness as a very singular creation. So singular, it was once cited by a Crown Court Judge in demonstration of a legal principle:

A man was on trial for giving spoons to a pawnbroker, representing them as being of the same quality as Elkington's A, or the very best in England at the time. In a question to counsel, Pollock, C. B., one of the judges, said:–
'Suppose a publican represents that his beer is not really Guinness, but equal to Guinness?'
(Extract from Regina *v.* Bryan case, 1857.)

So much for facts; as for fiction, Guinness has been well spoken of by many modern writers, including Dorothy L. Sayers (who, as will be seen later, had more than a passing interest in Guinness), Norah Hoult, Sir John Squire and Graham Greene who, in *Stamboul Train* (1932) has a character complain: 'No, I won't have any more of this foreign beer. My stomach won't stand it. Ask them haven't they got a Guinness. I'd just fancy a Guinness.'

In *Heart of the West*, the great American

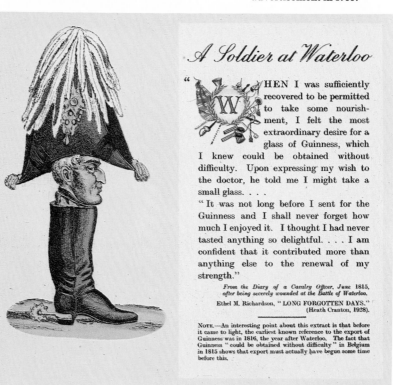

A Soldier at Waterloo

"WHEN I was sufficiently recovered to be permitted to take some nourishment, I felt the most extraordinary desire for a glass of Guinness, which I knew could be obtained without difficulty. Upon expressing my wish to the doctor, he told me I might take a small glass. ...

"It was not long before I sent for the Guinness and I shall never forget how much I enjoyed it. I thought I had never tasted anything so delightful. ... I am confident that it contributed more than anything else to the renewal of my strength."

From the Diary of a Cavalry Officer, June 1815, after being severely wounded at the Battle of Waterloo.
Ethel M. Richardson, " LONG FORGOTTEN DAYS."
(Heath Cranton, 1928).

NOTE.—An interesting point about this extract is that before it came to light, the earliest known reference to the export of Guinness was in 1816, the year after Waterloo. The fact that Guinness " could be obtained without difficulty " in Belgium in 1815 shows that export must actually have begun some time before this.

Even in central Asia

"...*I directed my attention to a wine and spirit store where I spied, greatly to my delight, the magic name of Guinness inscribed on imperial pints of stout. The price was stiff—eight shillings a bottle—but it didn't seem exorbitant when one considered the distance it had travelled from its native land. The stout was excellent.*"

"Innermost Asia" by R. P. Cobbold (Heinemann, 1900)

Everywhere, from China to Peru, there's nothing like a Guinness in sickness or in health. Wherever you are lucky enough to drink it, Guinness goodness never varies.

GUINNESS
IS GOOD FOR YOU

G.E. 1508 B

Penguinness

From an article by a member of Sir Douglas Mawson's Antarctic expedition of 1929.

"*The stores*" (left by Mawson's earlier expedition of 1911) "*were in good condition after 18 years; cocoa, salt, flour and matches from these stores were actually used afterwards ... There were also four bottles of Guinness on a shelf, which, although frozen, were put to excellent use.*"

The Belfast Telegraph, April 10th, 1933.

The goodness of Guinness is unaffected by climate. Wherever you drink it, in frozen north or sunny south, it always comes to you in the prime of condition.

GUINNESS
IS GOOD FOR YOU

G.E. 1509 B

Two press advertisements, illustrated by Ronald Searle (1949), showing something of Guinness's global reputation.

bringing up a bottle of Guinness. First rate for the nerves, sir; you'll want it.'

Not merely good for the nerves either, but excellent for education as one of A. J. Cronin's characters testifies in *Grand Canary* (1933): 'I got me eddication holdin' horses in Sackville Street, and learned me letters spellin' the Guinness's advertisements. Ye wouldn't believe it, me that reads Playto like a scholar.'

Plato himself had the misfortune to be born too soon in history, and was, therefore, denied the platonic friendship of Guinness. Similarly deprived was William Shakespeare who would surely have delighted in the drink's 'raven black' beauty. Certainly Hugh Kingsmill thought so when he wrote in 1936:

'Mine is a Guinness. And, by the way, what a splendidly shattering and satisfying sound those words have! If Shakespeare were alive today, as he unquestionably would be had he not been killed by his commentators, he could not find, and would be much too sensible to attempt to

find, any more royal and ringing opening to a sonnet than that which has just fallen from my – alas, only momentarily inspired – lips:

'Mine is a Guinness. Let no baser word
Profane the lips by Guinness once
bedewed.'

One poet who did rather more than merely 'bedew' his lips with Guinness, was Dylan Thomas: 'I remember once I drank forty-nine Guinnesses straight off and I came home on the top of a bus. Right on the top of the bus, too, not just the upper deck.' Which proves beyond doubt how good Guinness is for the nerves.

Finally, mention must be made of the high cultural status Guinness has achieved in its native land, where in the words of James Joyce (of whom more later) it is thought of as 'the country's wine'.

When, in 1837, the Dublin University Choral Society was formed, one of the rules laid down was that during meetings there should be 'a rest at 9 o'clock for half an hour when no refreshments will be allowed except Guinness and that the quantity be restricted to one bottle between every two persons present'. What joy – or despair – must have been caused by an odd-numbered attendance.

Irish novelist Brian O'Nolan ('Flann O'Brien') commemorated Guinness – or, as it was once known in Ireland, 'Plain' – in a poem in his 1939 work *At Swim-Two-Birds*. There is no better catalogue of the benefits of the brew:

When things go wrong and will not come
   right,
Though you do the best you can,
When life looks black as the hour of night –
A PINT OF PLAIN IS YOUR ONLY
   MAN.

When money's tight and is hard to get
And your horse has also ran,
When all you have is a heap of debt –
A PINT OF PLAIN IS YOUR ONLY
   MAN.

When health is bad and your heart feels
   strange,
And your face is pale and wan,
When the doctors say that you need a
   change –
A PINT OF PLAIN IS YOUR ONLY
   MAN.

When food is scarce and your larder bare
And no rashers grease your pan,
When hunger grows as your meals are
   rare –
A PINT OF PLAIN IS YOUR ONLY
   MAN.

In time of trouble and lousy strife,
You have still got a darlint plan,
You still can turn to a brighter life –
A PINT OF PLAIN IS YOUR ONLY
   MAN.

It must be said, nevertheless, that a pint (or two) of Plain can, sometimes, furnish the drinker with a somewhat disturbing vision of life, like that recorded by Edward Plunkett (Lord Dunsany) in his book *My Ireland*, and later adapted as a UK advertisement in 1955.

No writer has made more literary allusions to Guinness than James Augusta Joyce, which is some compensation for the fact that so many other eminent Irish men of letters – Swift, Goldsmith, Yeats, Wilde, Shaw and O'Casey – either didn't know about Guinness, or never got round to mentioning it. Although used in Irish Guinness advertising with sparing pride, Joyce's references to the drink have seldom appeared outside the Emerald Isle, presumably being thought too enigmatic for the average Guinness drinker in the United Kingdom. What would they make, for example, of such

O'Lara's Alarming Dream

"I'M WRITING a book about Ireland and they'll want to know what business the country does."
"Haven't we Guinness?" said O'Lara. "And what do we want with any more business than that? Don't they pay millions in taxes?"
And then a troubled look came over his face.
"Begob," he said, "I've nearly given up drinking it."
"Why's that?" I gasped.
"Because of a dream I had," said O'Lara, "after drinking no more nor a bottle. And then I went to bed and I had the dream."
"What was the dream?" I asked.
"Begob," he said, "It was terrible. I dreamed that I walked down to the shore of the sea one evening; I don't know what I was doing there, but I walked down to the shore; and it was somewhere near Dublin, for I could see the Wicklow mountains. And it wasn't night, for there was still some light in the sky; but it was getting late. And the shore was crowded with people all looking out to sea. And I said, 'What's the matter, boys?' And one or two of them answered, 'It is the end' and went on looking out to sea. So I looked too, in my dream. And I saw the horizon all dark with the smoke of ships, and the people staring at them as though the end of the world were there. 'Begob,' I said to myself, 'it's the English fleet, and those great big shells will be coming soon.'

"For the smoke was tearing up and the sky was black as thunder."
"'Is it the English fleet?'" I said.
"But they had all gone silent, and wouldn't speak any more.
"And then I saw that the ships were nearer than they looked in the evening. They weren't far away at all, and were quite small. And I took a man by the arm who was standing quite near me and I shook him, and said, 'Those little boats can't hurt us; sure, they're no bigger than Guinness' boats that do be on the Liffey.'
"And the man gave a great sigh and said, 'It is what they are.'
"And I cried out then, 'Ah, Boys, is it Guinness's going?'
"And I knew from the awful stillness that this was so.
"And I daren't have a sup of porter before going to bed anymore, for fear would I get that dream."
"Oh, I wouldn't bother," I said. "It was only a dream."
For he looked so doleful, I had to say something to try to cheer him.
"It isn't the dream I mind," he said. "But all the truth that there is in it."
From "My Ireland", by Lord Dunsany.

LORD DUNSANY was born in 1878 and succeeded his father as 18th Baron in 1899. He fought in the South African and First World Wars, and it was after the former that plays and tales in his highly personal, yet distinctively Irish idiom began to appear. He is among those who have tried to bring a more poetic diction to the stage, but it is perhaps his talent for the unlikely that has won him his widest public. Nothing could be more unlikely than O'Lara's dream.

A copy of this page may be obtained from Arthur Guinness, Son & Co. (Park Royal) Ltd., Advertising Dept., London, N.W.10

G.E. 2442.C

characters from *Finnegan's Wake* as Guinnghis Khan, Allfor Guineas, Ser Artur Ghinis or Mooseyeare Goorness? There are already more than enough people who don't know how to spell Guinness correctly, without making matters even more difficult.

The Joycean slogan 'Ghenghis is ghoon for you' may never have been used, but Guinness did once produce an advertisement in the United Kingdom which featured a *Finnegan's Wake* description of their beer as 'Foamous homely brew, bebattled by bottle, gageure de guegerre', even if they did ensure that it was accompanied by Mrs Carlyle and Mr Stevenson's rather more sober descriptions of the drink.

In Ireland, during the 1982 'Joycentenary', the Guinness Museum staged an exhibition entitled 'Wine of the Country', which took 'a James's gape at Guinness and Dublin'. The same year, Guinness's Irish advertising agency, Arks, produced a press advertisement celebrating Joyce's Guinnessisms.

In *Ulysses*, Joyce gives this description of how Lords Iveagh and Ardilaun ('Bungiveagh

Magazine advertisement using an extract from Lord Dunsany's *My Ireland*, illustrated by Charlton (1955).

and Bungardilaun') conducted the ritual of brewing Guinness:

> Terence O'Ryan heard him and straight way brought him a crystal cup full of the foaming ebon ale which the noble twin brothers Bungiveagh and Bungardilaun brew ever in their devine alevat, cunning as the sons of deathless Leda. For they garner the succulent berries of the hop and mass and sift and bruise and brew them and they mix therewith sour juices and bring the must to the sacred fire and cease not night or day from their toil, those cunning brothers, lords of the vat.

And, having enjoyed the handiwork of those lords, 'Guinness the free, the flow, the frothy freshener', most people's response is akin to that of the American writer Ray Bradbury who, in his short story 'The Anthem Sprinters', recalls sharing a round with convivial Irish company in Grafton Street's 'Four Provinces', after which . . .

'Licking the suds from our lips we regarded each other with benevolence.'

Any other emotion, of course, would be unpossible!

One final comforting thought: it comes from Rearden Conner's depressingly-titled novel, *I am Death*:

> 'Ah, the world's not such a bad place after all, Ma'am,' exclaimed Joe. 'Sure, there's many of the old sort left, an' they're still brewin' Guinness.'

Fifty years ago that was written, but to be sure isn't it still true today?

JAMES'S CHOICE

It has often been said that "James Joyce may have left Dublin - but Dublin never left James Joyce".

And even a cursory browse through his masterwork, Ulysses, will confirm the truth of that opinion. For in it Joyce deploys his prodigious knowledge of the city, its history and topography, with a fidelity to detail that is nothing short of astonishing.

Among the book's many references to Guinness, perhaps the most lyrical treats of the Guinness brothers, Lords Iveagh and Ardilaun, who "garner the succulent berries of the hop and bruise and brew them and mix therewith sour juices and bring the must to the sacred fire and cease not night nor day from their toil, those cunning brothers, lords of the vat".

Remembering the brewery barges, Joyce wrote of the days when as soon as one "set foot on O'Connell Bridge a puff ball of smoke plumed up from the parapet... brewery barge".

When it came to writing slogans Mr. Joyce was no slouch either. He suggested replacing "Guinness Is Good For You" with "Guinness - The Free, The Flow, The Frothy Freshener"!

Many changes have overtaken Dublin since the first Bloomsday in 1904, but the "frothy freshener" remains as good as ever.

And as good a way as ever to celebrate the day that's in it.

After all, one great original deserves another!

Guinness. No beer comes near.

Irish press advertisement celebrating James Joyce and his writings in praise of Guinness (1982).

JAMES'S GATE PORTER BREWERY, DUBLIN

GUINNESS & Co's DOUBLE STOUT

GUINNESS & Co's IN BOTTLE EXTRA STOUT

4

ADVERTISING IS GOOD FOR YOU

In the daily papers on the morning of 7 February 1929, a serious and rather pompous announcement appeared. With hindsight, this event was probably even more momentous than the author of this self-conscious piece of copy could have guessed. Certainly, advertising would never quite be the same again. The event was a milestone, but there had been a lot of up-hill walking before it had been reached.

THIS IS THE FIRST ADVERTISEMENT EVER ISSUED

in a national paper to advertise

GUINNESS

For over 150 years the House of Guinness have been engaged in brewing Stout. By concentrating upon doing one thing well, they have produced a beverage which stands alone.

Fortunes have been spent in study and development, going right back to the production of the kind of Barley seed that will enable the farmers to grow the Barley that makes the most suitable malt to make the best Stout.

As the result of quality, and quality alone, the Guinness Brewery has grown to be by far the largest in the world

ITS GREAT PURITY
Guinness is made solely from Barley Malt, Hops and Yeast, and is naturally matured. No artificial colour is added; the colour of Guinness is due to the roasting of the Barley.

ITS HEALTH-GIVING VALUE
Guinness builds strong muscles. It feeds exhausted nerves. It enriches the blood. Doctors affirm that Guinness is a valuable

restorative after Influenza and other weakening illnesses. Guinness is a valuable natural aid in cases of insomnia.

ITS NOURISHING PROPERTIES
Guinness is one of the most nourishing beverages, richer in carbo-hydrates than a glass of milk. That is one reason why it is so good when people are tired or exhausted.

 # GUINNESS
IS GOOD FOR YOU

Opposite: **Irish Showcards for public houses, 1868** (*top*) **and 1880.**
Above: **First UK press advertisement for Guinness, 7 February 1929.**
Above right: **Small-ad from** *The Morning Post* (1829), **used as part of a press advertisement one hundred years later.**

The only previous advertising for Guinness had been occasional references in press advertisements by suppliers or hoteliers; and, in Ireland, some point-of-sale advertisements – sometimes simply printed on card or paper, sometimes lavishly produced on glass or slate – for display in the bars of public houses.

GUINNESS'S DUBLIN STOUT.—This article is confidently recommended for home consumption and for export, and must, from its age, purity, and soundness, ensure the approbation and support of the Public. Sold in bottle and wood by Waring, Tuckett, and Foster, 79, Lower Thames-street; Ralph Milner, 4, Prospect-place, Southwark; W. Walker, 5, Fleet Market; Walwyn and Gayford, 7, Old Bond-street; M. B. Foster, 87, Wimpole-street; and Coleby and Long, 21, Bucklersbury.

But there was no advertising for Guinness in the United Kingdom, until the idea of a full-scale campaign emerged in the mid-twenties.

What is surprising, is that Guinness were so late upon the advertising scene. Since the turn of the century, advertising had played an increasingly important role in the commercial and industrial life of Britain, and many major companies – Cadbury, Kelloggs, Beechams, Pears and Gillette among them – had been advertising for twenty years or more.

Exactly why it took Guinness so long to see the light and start letting other people see the dark, is not easily explained. It has been suggested that Edward Cecil Guinness (who had successively been made Baronet, Baron, Knight of St Patrick, Viscount and Earl) would have found constant reminders of his 'trade' an embarrassment to his friends in social and royal circles. This view, however, was probably due to the attitude of his brother, Arthur, who had sold out his share in the brewery because, it is said, a labourer once pitched a sour bottle of Guinness over his Dublin garden wall with (to Lady Guinness's horror) much foul language.

It is more likely that Edward Guinness simply felt that the beer would always sell on its merits and didn't, therefore, need advertising.

What, then, brought about a change in this attitude during the twenties? To begin with, it is necessary to understand the position of Guinness within the British beer market. The majority of public houses were (as they still are) 'tied houses', that is, they were owned by a particular brewery and sold chiefly its own brews. Although Guinness owned no public houses, demand had meant that Guinness stout was, nevertheless, available in virtually every pub in the country. When, however, the beginnings of a trade depression started to adversely affect beer sales, competition between the breweries increased, and made life difficult for companies like Guinness who had no tied outlets for their product.

In 1926, Guinness saw an unprecedented levelling-off of sales, and it became evident that ways would have to be found to sustain and increase the public demand for Guinness.

Lord Iveagh, then aged 78, addressed himself to this problem and issued a clarion call to the Guinness board: 'I believe very firmly,' he said, 'that a business either goes forward or goes back – it seldom remains stationary – and when it arrives at that point, something ought to be done to get it moving again.'

Obviously, one solution was to advertise. Another reason for Guinness considering advertising at this time, was the possibility of opening a brewery in England. This was no new idea; in 1773, Arthur Guinness himself had considered establishing a brewery in Holyhead or Carnarvon in order to take advantage of the excise law in England and Wales and so undersell the Irish brewers. In 1912, Guinness had purchased a 100-acre site at Trafford Park in Manchester, and although that project was never developed, it was doubtless still a viable venture ten years later.

Advertising must, therefore, have been discussed in 1926, because just one year later, following the death of Lord Iveagh, Rupert Guinness started looking for a suitable advertising agency.

The new Lord Iveagh was adamant about one thing: if Guinness had to advertise, it must advertise well. After discussions and interviews with most of the leading advertising agencies (including J. Walter Thompson who later inherited the account), the Guinness Board appointed S. H. Benson Ltd., of Kingsway Hall, London.

Founded in 1893, by Samuel Herbert Benson, with Bovril as his first account, the agency had a reputation for clever advertising that used fine art work and punning copy. They had created the Mustard Club for Colmans, devised the slogan 'Prevents that sinking feeling' for Bovril, and had persuaded Macleans to allow them to change the pronunciation of the family name from 'Maclane' to 'Maclean' so they could use advertising copy that asked 'Have you Macleaned your teeth today?'

Samuel Benson died in 1914, two weeks before the outbreak of war, and was succeeded by his son, Philip de Gylpyn Benson, who left almost immediately to serve in the Navy. Invalided out in 1916, Philip Benson returned to take up management of the agency. An autocrat by nature, Benson ran the company with the tight discipline of a naval man-of-war. Many of his staff were, like him, former Senior Service men, and every morning he would drill the messenger-boys on the roof, just as Dorothy L. Sayers describes happening at the fictional advertising agency, Pym's (based on Bensons), in her novel *Murder Must Advertise*. It was Philip Benson who was in charge when the gentlemen from Guinness came to call.

Although Bensons must have been delighted at acquiring the Guinness account, it was, nevertheless, a somewhat daunting prospect, since Guinness already possessed a well-established image, which would have to be reflected in the advertising – if that advertising was going to be accepted as true.

Oswald Greene, a director of the agency and one of its best copywriters, began preparing a pilot campaign for Guinness. Greene, who had originated the Colman's Mustard Club as well as celebrated campaigns for Hennessy's Brandy and The Encyclopaedia Britannica, was a believer in what he described as 'reason why' copy – advertising that gave the consumer a good reason why he should buy. In the case of an already well-known product like Guinness, that reason should not conflict with whatever reasons consumers already had for buying it.

So, after a number of visits to the Guinness Brewery in Dublin where he studied every aspect of the beer's production, Oswald Greene set out to discover just what view of Guinness, Guinness drinkers had. He was assisted in this rudimentary market-research exercise by a junior copywriter, Bobby Bevan, who seventeen years later, would be chairman and managing director of Bensons.

Greene and Bevan's research largely consisted of visiting pubs and asking people why they drank Guinness. Again and again they received the same reply – they drank Guinness because it was good for them. So universal was this idea, Greene decided he need look no further for a copyline. 'Guinness' the advertisements would simply say 'is good for you'.

The Guinness Board, however, thought the idea too simple. What, after all, was the point of telling people something they already knew? That, of course, *was* the point. 'Guinness is good for you' would reinforce a commonly-held belief and confirm the motives of the regular Guinness drinker, while at the same

Edward Cecil Guinness, Lord Iveagh (1847–1927) (*top*); and Rupert Guinness, Lord Iveagh II (1874–1967), from a portrait by Guinness advertising artist, John Gilroy.

Above left: **Samuel Herbert Benson (1854–1914).**
Above: **One of the offices at S. H. Benson Ltd. Philip Benson is seated at the desk, centre.**
Left: **Messenger boys outside the entrance to S. H. Benson's offices in Kingsway Hall (*c* 1930).**

Robert 'Bobby' Bevan (1901–74), who began his career at S. H. Benson by writing copy for Guinness advertisements and went on to become chairman and managing director of the agency.

time offering non-Guinness drinkers a persuasive reason why they should try it.

It was decided to test the campaign in Scotland, and in January 1928, the first ever Guinness poster appeared.

It is doubtful whether, at the outset, there was much thought given to the truth of this statement, apart, of course, from the fact that Guinness contained only pure, natural ingredients. It was enough that people either already believed it to be true, or were prepared to believe it.

Having made the claim, however, Greene set about justifying it and produced seven reasons why Guinness was good for people. Guinness, it was said, was good for Strength, Nerves and Digestion, for Exhaustion and Sleeplessness, for its Tonic effects and for the Blood. Less reasons would have probably done just as well, and no doubt more could easily have been thought of, but – by intuition or design – Greene chose seven, a number that possessed a mystical ring of truth to it.

The Guinness Board were clearly committed to launching a national Guinness campaign, because the Scottish pilot advertising had hardly begun when, in March 1928, they appointed an advertising manager. The man chosen for the job was Martin Pick who had the charismatic connection of being the brother of Frank Pick, manager of the highly-acclaimed London Transport advertising.

Martin Pick spent five months in Dublin 'assimilating the brewery atmosphere' and then returned to London to open up an advertising office in St Paul's Churchyard from where he could co-ordinate the first English advertising campaign. At Bensons the lessons that were being learnt from the Scottish campaign were applied to the future plans that were being devised by Oswald Greene and the agency's art director, Dicky Richards.

The first Guinness poster to appear in Britain in the spring of 1929 was identical to that which had been used in Scotland a year earlier, and the designs which followed were equally as bold and direct, combining the 'good for you' slogan with a glass brimful of Guinness. In the autumn came a minor variation – 'It's Guinness, It's Good for You' – and an innovative poster using only the second half of that slogan and omitting the Guinness name, which indicates how swiftly 'Guinness is good for you' had achieved public recognition.

Not everyone was in favour of Guinness advertising. One member of the House of Lords, for example, complained of the proliferation of roadside hoardings, remarking that he couldn't go anywhere without seeing a poster which claimed that 'Guinness is good for you'. At which point in the debate, Lord Iveagh, then chairman of Guinness, rose to his feet and delivered the shortest speech ever made in the Lords: 'Guinness *is* good for you,' he said, and sat down.

As we have seen, the first press advertisement appeared in February, and its thickly-worded copy suggested that Guinness were rather trying to make up for lost time. A wide variety of advertisements followed: some stressed Guinness's longevity: 'Before Nelson – Before Napoleon – As long ago as 1778, the House of Guinness was brewing Guinness'; others concentrated on the mystique of Guinness brewing: 'If Genius is the infinite capacity for taking pains, the success of Guinness is explained.'

In the main, however, early advertising copy was concerned with supporting the fundamental idea that Guinness was good for you. The seven good reasons, first used in Scotland, were republished in the British press; and, on the poster hoardings, a new design gave an inspired twist to the campaign: 'A Guinness a day'.

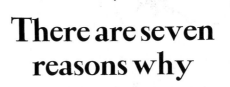

GUINNESS
is good for you

[NO. 7] FOR SLEEPLESSNESS

If you cannot sleep, try this simple remedy—a glass of Guinness at night. You will find it wonderfully soothing. GUINNESS brings natural sleep, and rebuilds the brain cells which have, through weakness, lost the power to rest.

GUINNESS is a naturally matured beverage. It comes rapidly to its best and needs no further keeping. Order Guinness frequently and do not keep it in a hot place.

Above: **One of the numerous variations on the 'Guinness is good for you' theme (*c.* 1930).**
Left: **Press advertisement, giving one of seven reasons why Guinness is good for you (1929).**
Opposite: **Guinness offers to keep the doctor away, on a 1929 poster.**

A
GUINNESS
A DAY

GUINNESS IS GOOD FOR YOU

The implication was obvious – 'A Guinness a day keeps the doctor away'. Today, this may seem an extraordinary claim for a beer advertisement, but seen in its context it is perfectly understandable. These were pre-National Health Service days, when there was a far greater incidence of illness and disease than is now known. A cursory glance at the advertisements in any popular newspaper will show just how many pills, potions and patent medicines were being sold. People were concerned with prevention of illness, and if an enjoyable beverage was also reckoned to help keep one fit it obviously had advantages over other drinks.

The idea, however, was not mere opportunism on the part of Guinness. Doctors already prescribed Guinness for nursing mothers and convalescents, and when Guinness decided to ask the medical profession what it thought about their stout, they received nothing but encouragement.

In 1906, a label was used in Liverpool for Foreign Export Stout which carried a testimonial from the vice-president of Dublin's Royal College of Surgeons:

> I have analysed a specimen of Messrs. A. Guinness, Son & Co.'s Foreign Export Stout ... It contains nearly seven per cent of solid matter in solution and is, therefore, a food as well as a stimulant and tonic. Charles A. Cameron, M.D.

From the thousands of doctors' letters Guinness extracted some compelling testimonials for use in advertising. Within a few months, Guinness had assumed the appearance of a modern-day cure-all. 'A bottle of Guinness,' said one doctor, 'has a wonderfully auto-suggestive cheer-producing effect!' More specifically, Guinness was good for anaemia, insomnia, neuralgia, post-influenzal debility and depression; it nourished brain-cells, 'prevented many people – especially business-men – from having a serious breakdown', provided 'a most valuable combined tonic and food for patients of the thin or emaciated kind', and it enabled those with chronic constipation to 'dispense with the usual artificial bowel-stimulation'.

In 1936, the Federal Alcohol Administration of America raised objections to the use of the slogan 'Guinness is good for you', on the grounds that it claimed a therapeutic value for Guinness which could not be proved. In response, Guinness prepared an impressive dossier of evidence to show that even if their beer wasn't therapeutic 'in the sense that it is a drug or medicine which has curative properties in specific diseases', it had – on the testimony of numerous doctors – 'certain qualities which make it "good for you" in many bodily conditions'.

This argument was then endorsed by fifty

Feels better, eats better, thinks cheerfully since the doctor ordered GUINNESS

"...I often prescribe Guinness, and for the following reason in chief. A bottle of Guinness put in front of, say, a dispirited, health-greedy convalescent has a wonderfully auto-suggestive cheer-producing effect. It looks potent and jolly and when consumed it acts as a stomachic and whip to the appetite. It makes the patient feel better and eat better and think cheerfully.

M.B., B.Ch.

Extract from one of the thousands of communications received by Messrs. Guinness from Doctors.

'GUINNESS IS GOOD FOR YOU'

facsimiles and transcripts of actual doctors' letters. Some showed rather more personal enthusiasm than sound medical reasoning: 'I think,' wrote one doctor, 'that Guinness is the best drink I've ever tasted!' Others were rather more specific in their analysis of the drink: 'It undoubtedly stimulates the secretion of milk in the breasts of nursing mothers'; 'I am sure it increases the activity of the Leucocytes (white cells) of the blood'; 'The finest tonic, stomachic and adjuvant to digestion we possess'; 'It ensures a good night's rest without recourse to drugs'.

'It is,' declared a doctor, whose letter was numbered 19102, 'the only form of alcohol I recommend'; while another (No. 27224), commented that 'though highly popular with

ESTD BLOOD. WOLFE & CO. 1850.

ROYAL COLLEGE OF SURGEONS, DUBLIN.

I have analysed a specimen of

Messrs. A. GUINNESS, SON & CO.'S FOREIGN EXPORT STOUT,

submitted to me for that purpose by Messrs. BLOOD, WOLFE and Co., Foreign Export Bottlers, Liverpool. I find it to be a perfectly pure article prepared only from malt and hops. It possesses in the highest degree the good qualities of Dublin Export Stout, and has evidently been brewed from the very best materials.

It contains nearly seven per cent. of solid matter in solution and is, therefore, a food as well as a stimulant and tonic.

CHARLES A. CAMERON, M.D.,
Vice-President Royal College of Surgeons, Ireland and Public Analyst for Dublin.

Above: **The tonic value of Guinness is attested to in this 1929 press advertisement.** *Left:* **A Guinness label used in Liverpool, bearing a testimonial from Dublin's Chief Health Officer (1906).**

all classes of the community, Guinness has not yet secured the unbounded popularity it deserves'. Which, of course, was the precise malaise which Guinness advertising was seeking to cure.

Under the British Code of Advertising Practice, Guinness would not now be permitted to claim health-giving qualities for the drink; nor, indeed, would they wish Guinness to have such a blatantly medicinal image. For almost forty years, however, it remained the ever-present foundation of Guinness advertising. Some temperance organisations objected – but most people happily accepted what Guinness and the doctors told them (it was, after all, only what they had always said themselves): Guinness *is* good for you.

The original slogan was used regularly on posters until 1937, after which it lingered on in different forms: in topical jokes about Guinness being good for 'u-nions' and for Nancy Mitford's 'U and Non-U' persons; in the acronym 'GIGFY', usually used in advertisements with sporting connections (including a crazy story about a whippet racer who christened his dog 'Gigfy'); and in the abbreviated slogan 'Good for You' which was used for advertisements in *Family Doctor* and other medical periodicals in the sixties. And even today, Guinness advertising overseas still uses 'Guinness is good for you' as one of its main slogans.

As late as the 1950s, doctors' testimonials were still being utilized, including (as a sign of the times) an increasing number of lady doctors, one of whom coyly wrote to say thankyou for 'the little fillip the Guinness fairy gives'!

Doctors, surgeons and nurses began writing their own Guinness jingles, rhymes and limericks:

Bedside
Canto

It doesn't matter what I've had
The patient said to me,
Your prescription for a Guinness is
the thing I like to see,
After rheumatism, chilblains,
meningitis, or the 'flu
It looks the same, it tastes the same,
it's just as Good for You.
So won't you keep your own good
health, and have a Guinness too?

M.B., CH.B.

And as late as 1968, a women's campaign was still claiming that 'A Guinness a day keeps the doctor away'. One of these advertisements (which showed ordinary mums and housewives coping with the ordinary pressures of everyday life), featured a lady who blithely declared: 'If I had my way Guinness would be on the National Health!'

GOOD FOR YOU

In 1984, Guinness produced a television commercial that jokingly returned to the medicinal image. 'A Guinness a day,' said the punchline 'keeps the *Guinnless* away.'

Although no one could have known it in 1928, Oswald Greene's simple idea was to become the most famous and enduring slogan in advertising history. There are no statistics to show the extent to which 'Guinness is good for you' was really common parlance in 1928; what is certain, however, is that Guinness advertising very quickly made it so.

There is an apocryphal story told in a variety of different versions by almost everyone who has ever worked at Guinness or in Guinness advertising: one man says to another man (or writes to the Brewery to say) that he considers the amount of money spent on Guinness advertising excessively wasteful, 'It doesn't make *me* drink Guinness!' he storms, '*I* drink it because it's good for you!'

It could almost be true! What's more, it could almost be an advertisement for Guinness!

43

Ten to one it's GUINNESS TIME

PRINTED IN GREAT BRITAIN BY THE DANGERFIELD PRINTING Cº Lᵀᴰ LONDON

5

ANY TIME IS GUINNESS TIME

Advertising, Guinness decided, was good for you, and the excellent reputation which they had rapidly established for themselves in the United Kingdom was to prove invaluable when, in 1932, they decided to proceed with plans for a Guinness Brewery in Britain. Although a prospective site existed in Manchester, Guinness chose instead a 126-acre site at Park Royal in North West London. The land was purchased in 1933 at a cost of approximately £1000 an acre. The identity of the purchaser was kept secret, and when building began, in 1934, there was much speculation as to the purpose of the huge factory that was springing up at Park Royal. In June of that year, the *Sunday Dispatch* confidently reported that the mysterious factory was a Government-owned fuel plant where alcohol was to be distilled from potatoes!

Eventually, the truth was revealed, and on 21 February 1936, the first Guinness brew in Britain was begun. By that time, Guinness advertising had been running for seven years, and was already developing into the idiosyncratic institution it eventually became. This had involved a cautious sophistication of the Guinness image, mainly achieved through the imaginative use of press advertising.

A poster, it has been said, is the visual equivalent of a shout, and the chief disadvantage of shouting is that it is rarely a subtle form of communication. The pages of newspapers and magazines, however, provide an opportunity for rather more relaxed conversation.

From the outset, Bensons decided that 'Guinness is good for you' should be augmented by other more informative and intriguing approaches to advertising.

The earliest of these, which had already been tried out in Scotland, concerned the colour of Guinness. Although in recent years the distinctive black-and-whiteness of Guinness has inspired a great deal of imaginative copywriting, in 1929 Guinness was pursuing an entirely different course. 'What colour is Guinness?' asked one press advertisement, followed a few days later by another which announced that 'The man who said *BLACK* was wrong', since Guinness was no more black than a black cherry was really black.

Opposite: **A poster celebrating Guinness meantime (1934).**
Right: **Decorations from press advertisements, comparing Guinness with black cherries and challenging drinkers to find the 'ruby glint' in their glasses (1929).**

Can you find THE RUBY in GUINNESS

For more than thirty years, Guinness advertising meant Gilroy advertising. His work is among the most widely recognised graphic art of the twentieth century, although, to many people, the artist himself is unknown.

John Gilroy, MA, ARCA, FRSA, was born in Newcastle-upon-Tyne in 1898. His father, John William Gilroy, was a technical draughtsman who turned to portrait and landscape painting. He instilled in his son – who showed an early aptitude for art – the essential importance and discipline of good drawing.

John studied art at Newcastle's King Edward VII School of Art, after which he was accepted to the Royal College of Art in London, although the First World War interrupted his studies and took him to France and the Middle East. Back in London at the end of the war, John returned to the Royal College and secured a Travelling Scholarship which enabled him to visit Europe and, in particular, to study the Italian masters.

John became a teacher at the Royal College, and spent some of his spare time designing poster advertisements. He joined the staff of S. H. Benson Ltd., in 1925, and began a long and successful career as one of the most gifted and imaginative artists in the history of British advertising.

John Gilroy's Guinness advertisements have not only won the affection of the public, they have earned the respect and admiration of fellow artists. When the engaging menagerie came to the attention of Walt Disney, he tried, unsuccessfully, to get Gilroy to go to Hollywood to work at his animation studio.

The personalities captured by Gilroy in his Guinness characters (the secret of their success is always to be found in the drawing and placing of the eye), is evidence of his astute observation. It is that quality as an observer that has made Gilroy one of Britain's most successful portrait painters. His subjects over the years have included Her Majesty Queen Elizabeth and many other members of the Royal Family, Lords Mountbatten and Alexander, Sir Winston Churchill, Edward Heath, Pope John and a troupe of theatrical knights including Wolfit, Clements and Gielgud.

Whether he is painting the Queen Mother, a Guinness ostrich or one of the many whimsical designs created for Royle's greetings cards, Gilroy is a highly creative and disciplined artist.

In 1976, John Gilroy received an Honorary MA from the University in his home town of Newcastle-upon-Tyne.

Good for you, Gilroy

Whats the TIME?

Left: **Scraperboard illustration by Gilroy as part of the 'Guinness Time' campaign (1936). It appeared in newspapers, running the length of one whole column.** *Right:* **Poster (1931).**

After Work is
GUINNESS TIME
GUINNESS IS GOOD FOR YOU

Time you came down
GUINNESS TIME

Guinness, it was revealed, was actually 'ruby-coloured' – so began a long and curious campaign in which Guinness was poetically described as being 'more precious than rubies', 'a jewel of a drink', which invited the drinker to try and find the ruby in *his* glass of Guinness.

Instructions were even provided: 'Hold it up to a strong light, slightly above your eyes, and round the base of the glass you will see a thin bright gleam of ruby light.' More complex arrangements were also devised for the home experimenter, such as half-filling a glass with Guinness and inserting an inverted wine-glass (being careful to keep the air trapped within the bowl), then – when raised to the light – 'you will see the hollow of the wine-glass suffused with a deep ruby glow'.

Some artwork depicted an actual ruby gleaming away in the bottom of the glass, and it is possible that this campaign gave rise to the legend that diamond prospectors in Africa used Guinness to test the genuineness of a

gem, since only a true diamond was able to shine through the Guinness darkness – inferior stones, presumably, being totally outshone by all those rubies.

Although there was a vague attempt to relate the ruby gleam to the quality of Guinness – it was the result of roasting barley; it was a sign of purity – the campaign dubiously promoted Guinness as a kind of novelty drink, rather as happened, some years later, when drinkers were invited to inscribe their initials on the head of a Guinness.

As Guinness advertising got into its stride the personalities of the people behind it became increasingly evident; so much so, that in the spring of 1930, just one year after advertising had begun, the first Guinness joke was born. It showed a glass of Guinness amongst a row of other famous heads.

The artist was John Gilroy who had already painted the endless line-up of Guinness glasses that had been appearing on the first posters. Gilroy now considers the design rather less than satisfactory – particularly the caricatured features of the Guinness-fancier – but it was, nevertheless, the first flicker of a Guinness

GUINNESS TIME

How doth the goodly Guinness glass
    Improve each dining hour!
No other drink is in its class
    For strength and staying-power.

How cheerfully it seems to grin,
    How creamily it flows!
How does that ruby gleam get in?
    Ah, Guinness only knows!

With acknowledgments to Isaac Watts and Lewis Carroll.

smile, and a prelude to thirty years of classic Gilroy posters.

Although the new poster drew attention to the famous Guinness head, the predominant concern of the copy was still its goodness. Now the trouble with being told that things are good for you, is that experience indicates that the ratio of their goodness is likely to be in direct proportion to their unpleasantness! Guinness could not afford to be thought of as tasting like spinach or sal volatile, so Bensons began showing Guinness as an appealing and enjoyable drink as well as being beneficial. The next poster reverted to the familiar glass, but this time with a hand about to grasp it, and the caption: 'I'm simply longing for a Guinness'. It went on, for the first time, to describe Guinness as 'strengthening'.

Guinness advertising was on the brink of moving towards an entirely new campaign that was to provide their second great slogan: 'Guinness for Strength'. During the next few years, two other major campaigns were begun – one was to feature clever literary parodies, in particular of the works of Lewis Carroll; the other introduced the world to the famous Guinness animals and their tormented keeper. These three campaigns will be examined in greater detail later, here we will concentrate on some of the many other ingenious ideas that came – and sometimes went – on the posters and in the press during the pre-war years.

In 1931, a neon-sign in Piccadilly Circus began flashing the news that Guinness was good for you. The sign was quickly followed by an electric illuminated clock, and Guinness Time had been discovered.

Guinness clocks were erected in several major cities in Britain, and people were soon arranging to meet one another 'Under the Guinness clock'. Guinness Time posters began with a simple clock-face, the hands on which pointed to one o'clock. Other variations on this theme included 'ONE – and all say Guinness Time', 'Lunch Time is Guinness Time', 'Home by Guinness Time', and 'It strikes one it's Guinness Time'.

The Guinness Time theme successfully transferred to the press with a variety of new clock captions – 'Hands up for Guinness', 'High Time I had my Guinness' – and it also inspired some of Benson's earliest rhyming advertisements:

When I sat on my Father's knee,
He used to show his watch to me;
He made the gold 'Repeater' chime
And then he said 'It's Guinness Time'.

So when I see a clock today,
I think of what he used to say:
'When I'm run down I've always found
Guinness makes the wheels go round'.

There's nothing like a GUINNESS

Two years later the clock-face reappeared on the posters, this time made more whimsical by the addition of a small – but quite expressive – pair of eyes.

The anthropomorphic clock-face had been preceded by a similarly transformed Guinness head. Although the glasses which appeared on the posters were always painstakingly painted and printed, they looked, perhaps, a little daunting and unapproachable. What better way to make Guinness look more inviting than to develop that early Gilroy joke about the Guinness head? If it had a head – it obviously followed that it must also have a face.

As we shall see, the face on the glass was to linger into the fifties, and had a tiresome, but thankfully short-lived, career on television. In

Opposite: **The Guinness head and the clock face eye each other up on this 1936 London Underground poster, parodying Lewis Carroll's own parody of Isaac Watts.** *Above:* **The anthropomorphic pint, used on a poster in 1933.**

You'll feel *fresher* when you've had a Guinness

Fresh as a Daisy!

the 1930s, however, when three million people were unemployed, and life for many Britons was far from bright, the smiling Guinness face had a welcome cheerfulness whenever it appeared.

When the Guinness face was next seen on the outdoor hoardings, it was accompanied by a new slogan: 'There's nothing like a Guinness'. Nor, of course, is there – except, as a subsequent copyline pointed out, 'another Guinness'!

The uniqueness of Guinness was a recurrent topic: 'All cats are alike in the dark – but even in the dark you could not mistake a Guinness for anything else, or anything else for a Guinness'. Which is how Guinness came to coin the term 'unmistakability'. The advertising was equally unmistakable, with its tortuous puns – 'Beauty and the Yeast' and 'Yule make life brighter with Guinness' – and its terrible music-hall gags such as: 'I feel like a Guinness.' 'I wish you were!'

"*I feel like a Guinness.*"
"*I wish you were!*"

Have a glass·of
GUINNESS
when you're <u>Tired</u>

"How do you keep Guinness in the home?"

"We don't—we drink it!"

Any cool place will do for your Guinness—except a refrigerator. To enjoy Guinness in its creamy perfection, order in small quantities: a week's supply at a time. Because Guinness is both invigorating and refreshing, you feel you've had something worth drinking when you've had a Guinness.

GUINNESS
IS GOOD FOR YOU

Order Half-a-dozen for the Home

One of the most successful of the thirties campaigns was 'Have a glass of Guinness when you're tired', which introduced the idea that Guinness had restorative qualities and which provided seemingly limitless opportunities for visual and verbal gags, including games, rhymes, puzzles and shaggy-dog stories.

Eventually the slogan became so well known that Gilroy was able to produce a 'tired' cartoon and omit the caption (right). The only reference to Guinness, it should be noted, is on the escalator advertisements.

Another design by Gilroy parodied the work of Henry Moore. The poster was never put into production, but Gilroy was used to ideas not being accepted. He jokingly recalls, for example, how one of his most inventive slogans was rejected: 'Guinness makes loose women tight!'

An idea that was submitted by several members of the public followed a news story about the sighting of a seal off the coast of Britain. The unfortunate animal was trapped in an old car tyre, and it was suggested that a picture of the seal should be used with the slogan: 'Have a Guinness when you're tyred'!

In 1933, a major press campaign was launched to promote Guinness take-home sales, using distinctive art-work by Gilroy and H. M. Bateman who took up the campaign with a series of drawings depicting the eccentric places where people kept Guinness within the home. In addition to cellars and under-

They've been waiting for that Guinness at No. 11

The way to enjoy your Guinness in the best condition is to order a week's supply to be sent round regularly. Keep it ready to hand in a coolish place and take one every day for vitality and strength. They will tell you at No. 11—and doctors will tell you the same—that both body and nerves are braced by a daily Guinness.

And as you yourself know, you feel you've had something worth drinking when you've had a Guinness.

A GUINNESS A DAY IS GOOD FOR YOU

Order half-a-dozen for the Home

Left: **Two 1933 press advertisements by H. M. Bateman and John Gilroy.** *Below:* **A caption-less Gilroy advertisement (1936).** *Opposite:* **An illustration by Bateman (1935).**

Have a glass of Guinness
when you're <u>Tired</u>

G.E.677

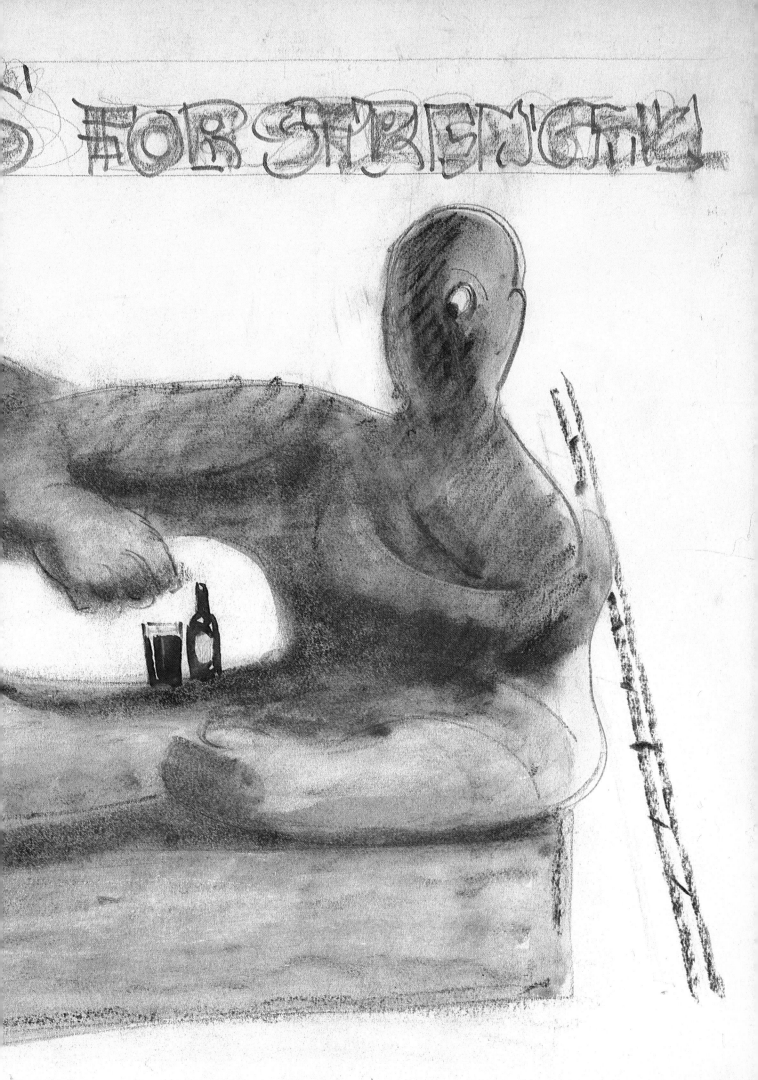

Umpire: "Will you take middle or leg, Sir?"

Batsman: "I think I had better take a GUINNESS!"

stair cupboards, people were seen stashing it away inside ming vases, grandfather clocks and grand pianos.

Bateman also produced a series of sporting cartoons in the style of his famous pictures about The Man Who.... These timorous little sportsmen were early examples of what Guinness advertising was later to call 'The Guinnless'.

It is difficult to realise just how innovatory much of the early Guinness advertising was. For example, they were probably the first advertiser to show evidence of their product's consumption by depicting a recently-drained glass. Its purpose was obvious – if the sight of a glass of Guinness provided an incentive, how much more so the sight of one that has just been enjoyed by someone else.

It was enough to make you want to empty a few glasses yourself! Providing, that is, you weren't one of those poor fish who never had a Guinness.

The one drink the bootleggers couldn't copy

Enjoy Dublin's world-famous brew

Guinness were exporting stout to the USA as early as 1849, and have gone on doing so ever since – except for the prohibition years, 1920–33. Following the repeal of the prohibition, Guinness began advertising in America, with such copy lines as: 'The Return of an Exile!' and 'The One Drink the Bootleggers couldn't copy', and useful hints on pronouncing Guinness for the benefit of a 'young man at Yale', who wasn't sure if it was Jinniss, Gwinnis, Jiness or Gwinness.

'There's gold' (not rubies, you notice) 'in those bottles!' declared one trade advertisement, and extensive space was taken in the press to promote Guinness as an accompaniment to oysters and Thanksgiving turkeys ('A Guinness with every gobbler'). Of great importance also was the drink's Irish heritage. As one advertisement boldly put it – '4,000,000 Irishmen can't be wrong!'

American press advertisements (*clockwise*): 1939, 1940, 1941, 1949.

6

ADVERTISING FOR STRENGTH

'What Guinness poster do you remember best?' Whenever researchers have asked that question, they have nearly always received the same answer: 'The man with the girder.' It is the most famous Guinness poster of all time, and one of the undisputed masterpieces of advertising art. This poster, painted by John Gilroy, first appeared in 1934, and represents the creative peak of the 'Guinness for Strength' campaign which had begun six years earlier with one of the Scottish pilot posters bearing the slogan 'Guinness is so strengthening'.

In the United Kingdom, Guinness's ability to give strength was the very first of the 'Seven Good Reasons why Guinness is Good for You': 'It strengthens your muscles for play; it strengthens you for work; it strengthens your nerves and digestion.' The campaign evolved as the result of a feeling that 'Guinness is good for you' appealed mainly to women. 'Guinness for Strength', it was thought, would offer a masculine balance to the advertising. Certainly, in the early years, the two themes alternated on the hoardings.

The first appearance of the 'Strength' slogan on a UK poster was in 1930.

Designed by the distinguished German artist Ludwig Hohlwein, it showed an elderly man holding out his hand towards a glass of Guinness, as if extolling its virtues. This was the first and only 'serious' representation of a Guinness drinker to appear on a poster until 1963. Although a powerful design, with a subtle implication of strength of character, it was, presumably, not considered particularly successful, since the slogan completely disappeared from posters for the next two years.

The first 'Guinness for Strength' press advertisement appeared in 1929, and featured the famous eighteenth-century pugilists Mendoza and Humphreys. Obviously the idea was too aggressive to be compatible with the Brewery's mainstream advertising.

John Gilroy began experimenting with humorous applications of the 'Strength' slogan, his first design depicting a pair of sedan-chair-men stopping off at a pub for a little strength. The idea was rejected, but his

Opposite: **A preliminary sketch for the 'girder' poster by John Gilroy (1934).**

Above: **The first 'Guinness for Strength' poster by Ludwig Hohlwein (1930).**
Right: **Press advertisement (1929).**

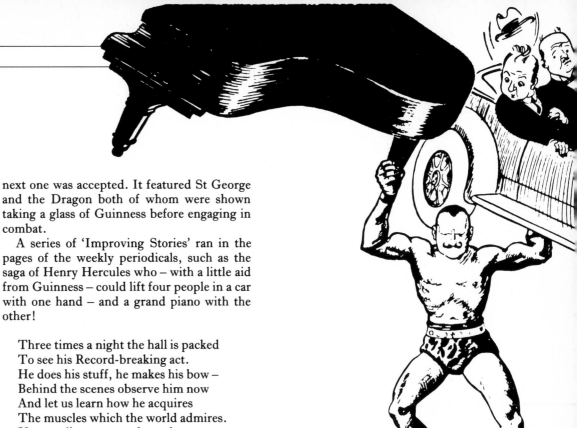

next one was accepted. It featured St George and the Dragon both of whom were shown taking a glass of Guinness before engaging in combat.

A series of 'Improving Stories' ran in the pages of the weekly periodicals, such as the saga of Henry Hercules who – with a little aid from Guinness – could lift four people in a car with one hand – and a grand piano with the other!

> Three times a night the hall is packed
> To see his Record-breaking act.
> He does his stuff, he makes his bow –
> Behind the scenes observe him now
> And let us learn how he acquires
> The muscles which the world admires.
> Upon a silver tray are brought
> A glass and bottle; as I thought,
> His secret stands revealed at length
> Guinness – the sovereign source of
>   strength.

Gilroy's first successful poster design on the 'strength' theme appeared in the summer of 1932, and featured a little man with the job of statue-cleaning. The amusing notion of a workman needing a Guinness in order to find the strength for the herculean task of cleaning a statue of Hercules made this a popularly-appreciated comic poster.

Gilroy made detailed anatomical studies for the statue, which (he jestingly adds) was inspired by his own titanic torso!

Above left: **John Gilroy's first attempt at a 'Guinness for Strength' advertisement, which was rejected.**
Below left: **Gilroy's second – acceptable – design, used in all the major illustrated papers (1930).**
This page: **Decorations by Gilroy to the saga of Henry Hercules (1931).**

The poster's success led to the story behind the poster being told – in verse, naturally:

> There was a little man, and he had a little
>   job,
> It was cleaning up the statues of the great,
> Such as Moses and Lord Byron, the
>   Discobolus of Myron,
> William Pitt, and other pillars of the State.
>
> From twelve o'clock to one he would take a
>   little rest,
> With his back against Diana's marble
>   knees,
> Or propped against Disraeli, he'd consume
>   in peace his daily
> Glass of Guinness with a bit of bread and
>   cheese.
>
> One lunch time as he sat at the feet of
>   Hercules
> In a *dolce far niente* sort of way,
> Some people praised the statue, and said
>   'What a pity that you
> Never see such strength and energy
>   to-day!'
>
> Then up rose the little man, seized the
>   statue round the leg –
> And lifted it, as easy as could be!
> And pointing to the bottle, he cried
>   'GUINNESS! that is what'll
> Make you all as strong as Hercules and
>   me!'

It was now firmly established that a glass of Guinness – like Popeye's can of spinach – could enable the most astounding feats of superhuman strength. A new poster design, showing a workman leaning rather too heavily on a pillar of St. John's, Covent Garden, appeared the following spring, and July 1934 saw special posters and press advertisements, commemorating the demolition of the old Waterloo Bridge.

It was perhaps because of this contemporaneous advertisement, that Guinness briefly considered the possibility of purchasing Waterloo Bridge and re-erecting it at the site of the brewery then being built at Park Royal, where it was thought it might span the underground railway line and connect Western Avenue with the main gate in Coronation Road. The idea was eventually discounted as being too costly, and too likely to generate fresh press enquiries into the secret potato distillery!

A few months later, the celebrated girder-carrier made his appearance. While Gilroy was designing the poster, his son – who was training to become a civil engineer – pointed out that the girder in the draft drawing was placed in a position that couldn't possibly have balanced in real life. It might be thought that 'real life' was scarcely a relevant factor when one considered the idea of a man carrying a forty-foot girder on his head, but Gilroy adjusted his design nevertheless to achieve the illusion of a perfect balance.

The poster was a triumph. So much so that people ordering Guinness in pubs took to asking for a Girder; and years later, applicants for jobs at the Guinness Brewery were still being told that the first test of their suitability was to see if they could pick up and carry a girder!

David Ogilvy, the grand panjandrum of advertising, believes that this and Gilroy's other 'strength' posters have never been excelled anywhere in the world.

Why then was the poster so phenomenally successful? It was due, in part, to a basic concept that was so outrageous it caught the public's imagination, but it was also due to Gilroy's bold composition – the man's jaunty walk and blissful expression, and the effortless way in which he carried the metallic bulk of the girder.

As a piece of design for a large-scale poster it was superb – a dynamic shape, silhouetted against a white background, that was easily identified during the day or at night by the casual observer or the passenger on a passing bus.

So strong and so lasting was the impression created by the poster, that people who weren't born when it first appeared on the hoardings still have an astonishing awareness of the design. In fact, Jeremy Bullmore of J. Walter Thompson, who reintroduced the girder-man

in 1976, believes the poster's lasting popularity might well be evidence for the existence of 'pre-natal advertising recall'!

Christmas 1934 saw the first parody of the girder poster – drawn, of course, by Gilroy! It showed Santa Claus carrying a huge Christmas tree just as the workman had carried the girder. *The Advertising World* called it a 'design-in-a-hundred'.

A tree provided the idea for Gilroy's next 'strength' poster in 1937, a design which caused a minor public controversy – always a useful aid to an advertising campaign – when

Above: **Life-study by Gilroy for his 1932 'Strength' poster** (*opposite*).
Overleaf: **The man carrying the girder first appeared on posters in 1934.**

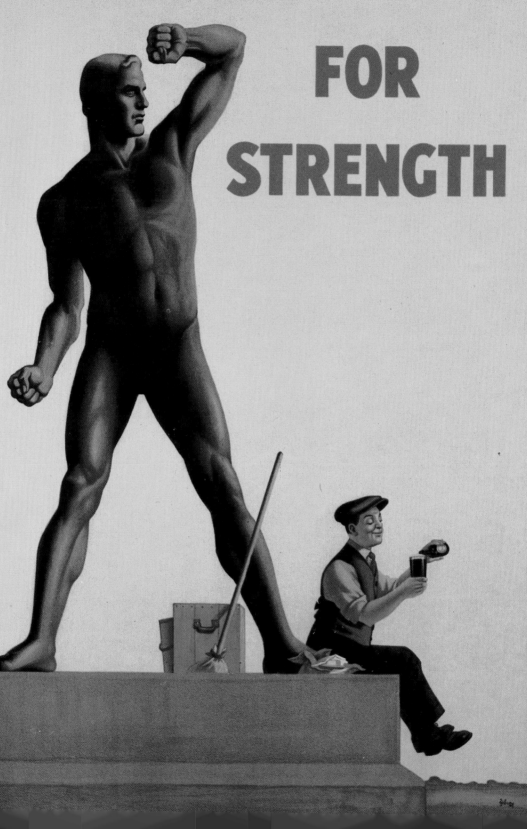

S

FOR
STRENGTH

people wrote to Guinness to say that the artist had made the appalling blunder of drawing the lumberjack's axe the wrong way round! Nobody, it should be noted, wrote to protest that it was impossible to fell so large a tree with one swing – merely that the blunt side of the axe had been used!

Elaborate plans were drawn up and sent to correspondents, and advertising manager Martin Pick kept an axe in a corner of his office in order to demonstrate the accuracy of Gilroy's picture whenever doubts were raised – and, perhaps, to threaten those who persisted!

The lumberjack advertisement was revived in the press during the fifties, this time with a piece of doggerel added:

The Woodman does not spare this tree;
Mark how he set about it.
'Guinness for Strength' his rule must be –
What would men do without it?

Many other potential ideas were thought up to utilize the 'strength' slogan. Among the designs sketched out by Gilroy, but finally rejected, were a park-keeper carrying two towering piles of stacking-chairs to a bandstand; a man pulling a lifeboat ashore, single-

WATERLOO BRIDGE is coming down

Guinness for Strength

Left: **Press advertisement celebrating the demolition of Waterloo Bridge (July 1934).**
Below: **The porters of Covent Garden feature on this 1933 poster, recalling Guinness's long association with the porterage trade.**
Opposite: **Gilroy provided this seasonal imitation of his famous girder poster.**

No words are needed ; for the picture tells
    What happens when, with one gigantic hand
This modern Samson negligently fells
    A serviceable building near the Strand.

Draining his glass of Guinness, he enjoys
    The vision of his nervous mate's distress
And—while it is a pillar he destroys,
    He makes a column—for the Daily Press.

The fact that strength like this is very rare
    Does not affect the moral of this rhyme ;
"Guinness for Strength" wins plaudits
                everywhere—
    In fact, it "brings the house down"
                every time !

GUINNESS FOR STRENGTH

G.E. 329 B.

CHRISTMAS IS COMING

GUINNESS
FOR STRENGTH

GUINNESS
FOR STRENGTH

PRINTED IN GREAT BRITAIN BY JOHN WADDINGTON LTD., LEEDS.

Opposite: **The controversial lumberjack poster (1937). Is he holding the axe the wrong way round?**
Above and right: **Two unused 'Guinness for Strength' designs by Gilroy (c 1938).**
Top right: **'I'd give the world for a Guinness', from a Gilroy magazine advertisement (1934).**

handed; a ship-builder running down the slipway to launch a liner; a builder putting the roof on a house, and a bottle of Guinness holding up one end of a suspension bridge.

The campaign remained a regular feature of Guinness advertising during the war, throughout the post-war years, and, indeed, well into the sixties. Today it lives on in the 'Guinness for Power' slogan which is widely used in overseas advertising. In a wider context, 'Guinness for Strength' introduced the idea of using comic hyperbole in advertising, and a great many advertisers have subsequently made hyper-extravagant claims for their products that are allowable under current advertising codes simply because of their sheer impossibility. Most notable of such campaigns have been the vintage 'Double Diamond works wonders' advertisements, the long-running 'Heineken refreshes the parts other beers can't reach' (which once parodied the Gilroy girder poster), and the more recent campaign featuring the titanic accomplishments of the man who drinks Carling Black Label.

Mackeson stout, which in the sixties cashed in on the Guinness reputation for goodness with the slogan: 'Looks good, tastes good, and, by golly, it *does* you good!', recently adopted the strength theme and showed an elephant being pulled along by an anthropomorphic bottle, accompanied by the revised – code-dodging – slogan: 'By golly...'

Familiarity with the 'Guinness for Strength' slogan and its successors makes it difficult to appreciate just how inspired was this campaign. Not only did it claim special – very masculine – properties for the drink, it also set Guinness totally apart from other drinks, thereby reinforcing the whole concept of its uniqueness. The kind of drink a man would give the world for!

In the 40 years following his first appearance, John Gilroy's girder-man has been seen in a variety of guises, of which these are just a few...

My Goodness My Girder!

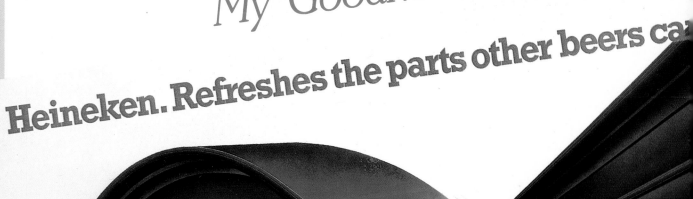

Heineken. Refreshes the parts other beers ca

ARTHUR GUINNESS SON & CO LTD.

MY GOODNESS
we must speed up!

Bigger production is good for you

G.E.1442.B

MILLION
GUINNESS
for strength every day

Strube applies a famous Guinness poster to everyday life

CARRYING ON

CARRYING girders may not be much in your line —
but you've some pretty heavy burdens, haven't you?
The housework; shopping; the washing; a working
day at desk or bench. And those are the very things
that Guinness helps you to bear.

Guinness is richly invigorating. Its taste is truly
refreshing because it's such a *clean* taste. Even the
look of a Guinness makes life seem brighter! And it's
good for you.

GUINNESS
for strength

Clockwise:
Imitation is the sincerest form of flattery:
Gilroy's powerful image borrowed by that other imaginative advertiser,
Heineken, to promote lager rather than stout (1977)

J. Walter Thompson bring back the girder (1976)

Harold Wilson and George Brown, as seen by cartoonist Vicky (1965)

A domestic girder-carrier by Strube (1955)

Gilroy puts the girder into shape for a new poster (1960)

The girder-man joins the National Productivity Drive (1947).

Guinness.
It's as long as you can remember.

Bottle Royal

(With acknowledgments to Macmillan & Co.,Ltd.)

Gilroy

"What are the Lion and the Unicorn fighting for?" said Alice.

"They both want a Guinness," said the King, "and there's only one left."

"Does the one that wins get the Guinness?" asked Alice.

"Dear me, no!" said the King. "The one that's had the Guinness wins."

GUINNESS IS GOOD FOR YOU

GUINNESS IN WONDERLAND

White Rabbits, Mad Hatters and Cheshire Cats talking all manner of nonsense about Guinness. On the face of it, it was rather odd. S. H. Benson had swiftly and firmly established Guinness as being refreshing, strengthening and good for you. In the beginning, Guinness advertising had meant a serious-looking (one might even say, sober) glass of Guinness. Eventually, some light relief had arrived with Gilroy's strong-men – working-class characters with a down-to-earth, variety hall, sense of humour. Then, suddenly, Guinness advertising went off in a quite unprecedented direction. Advertisements were being peopled by a little girl called Alice and her bizarre companions from Wonderland. It was just as if the solidly-lettered Guinness name had gone berserk and started growing curlicues.

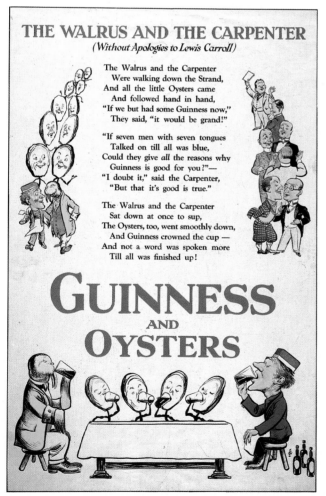

THE WALRUS AND THE CARPENTER
(Without Apologies to Lewis Carroll)

The Walrus and the Carpenter
Were walking down the Strand,
And all the little Oysters came
And followed hand in hand,
"If we but had some Guinness now,"
They said, "it would be grand!"

"If seven men with seven tongues
Talked on till all was blue,
Could they give *all* the reasons why
Guinness is good for you?"—
"I doubt it," said the Carpenter,
"But that it's good is true."

The Walrus and the Carpenter
Sat down at once to sup,
The Oysters, too, went smoothly down,
And Guinness crowned the cup —
And not a word was spoken more
Till all was finished up!

GUINNESS
AND
OYSTERS

For all their exotic frivolity, the literary parodies – of which the Alice advertisements were by far the most popular – had an important effect on Guinness advertising. They widened its scope, showed it to be capable of subtlety, as well as broad humour, and won the affection of the littérateur and the juvenile. It must be said, of course, that neither featured heavily as Guinness drinkers, but the goodwill and publicity it gave the drink were immensely valuable. In addition, the association with as unique a work as *Alice's Adventures in Wonderland* served to underline the uniqueness of Guinness, and Gilroy always ensured that the product was very much in evidence. How much of all this was intended by Bensons is impossible to say, although they could scarcely have been unaware of the family-appeal which the advertising had. Today, of course, such an approach to advertising would be quite unacceptable.

It all began with oysters. Guinness and oysters have always gone together like strawberries and cream or (in the words of an American Guinness advertisement) like 'waffles and syrup or corned beef and cabbage'.

The copywriting department at Bensons – then known as the 'Literary Department' – seeking a suitable way to advertise Guinness and oysters, hit upon the idea of using the story of the Walrus and the Carpenter from Lewis Carroll's *Through the Looking-Glass*. When one remembers that most of Benson's copywriters were highly educated university men and women, such an opportunity to use a well-known, well-loved work of literature was practically irresistible. Among those who were writing copy at Bensons in those days were Cecil Woodham-Smith, Dorothy L. Sayers, Pamela Frankau, Tim Milne (A.A.'s nephew), Michael Barsley (later a BBC radio producer and the author of two books of *Alice* parodies) and Ronald Barton (an accomplished former actor and BBC scriptwriter).

At the end of the first year's advertising, in December 1929, a press advertisement appeared featuring the Walrus and the Carpenter and their hapless victims, the oysters. The verses were by Ronald Barton, and the illustrations (in the style of John Tenniel's originals) were by Gilroy.

The books written by the Reverend Charles Lutwidge Dodgson under the name 'Lewis Carroll' have probably been more frequently parodied than any other work of literature, which is interesting when one considers that much of what he wrote was parody to begin with. Many of Carroll's verses are themselves pastiches of Victorian parlour poetry, now largely unknown in their original form. One such poem, written by Robert Southey in 1799, is 'The Old Man's Comforts and How He Gained Them', which Carroll re-wrote in 1864 as 'You Are Old Father William', and which either Ronald Barton or Bobby Bevan re-wrote with a Guinnessy slant in 1931. Courteous to the last, Guinness apologised to both previous versifiers.

If ever a Guinness advertising idea was fortuitously timed, it was their 'Alice' campaign, for 1932 saw the centenary of Lewis Carroll's birth and a revival of interest in his work. A major Lewis Carroll exhibition was held in London organized by a committee whose members included Sir James Barrie, A. A. Milne, E. V. Lucas, Sir Gerald Du Maurier and Dame Madge Kendal, and the 80-year-old Alice Hargreaves (Lewis Carroll's original muse) was honoured and fêted in both America and the United Kingdom. The ever-present gloom of the early thirties was relieved by a charmingly eccentric outbreak of Carrollian euphoria, of which Guinness were accidentally a part. Although they omitted to produce an advertisement marking the centenary, plenty of other Carrollian inventions appeared in the press during the next few years.

In June 1933, the first colour advertisement to appear in a newspaper was published in the *Daily Express*. The advertiser was Guinness and it featured the lobster from *Wonderland* together with a parody of Lewis Carroll's parody of Isaac Watts!

When Bensons first sent Alice through the Guinness-glass, neither Lewis Carroll's stories nor John Tenniel's illustrations were in the public domain. Macmillan & Company, who published the *Alice* books, were none too pleased to find Carroll's heroine endorsing stout, and considered Guinness and Gilroy to have infringed their copyright. Eventually, however, the matter was amicably settled over a crate or two of Guinness, and the collaboration continued – to everyone's satisfaction, since the parodies not only helped boost sales of Guinness, but also of Lewis Carroll's books.

A year or two after the campaign began, Guinness decided to publish its own Alice book. It was designed to be given away as a Christmas greeting to the Brewery's longstanding friends in the medical profession. Ever since Guinness had first circularised doctors in 1929, and had begun using their testimonials, they had had excellent relations. Blood-donor centres were given free supplies of Guinness and general practitioners were invited to recommend patients whom they considered would benefit from taking a glass of stout – each such patient received half-a-dozen bottles (as did some of the doctors who protested that they were the ones who needed a Guinness).

A Christmas booklet, which wittily reminded the recipient of the goodness of Guinness, would be a useful – and not very expensive – public-relations exercise. *The Guinness Alice* was published in December 1933, and

FATHER WILLIAM
(With apologies to Lewis Carroll & Robert Southey)

"You are old, Father William," the young man said,
  "And yet you're remarkably fit,
You sleep from the moment you get into bed,
  Which is rare at your age, you'll admit."

"In my youth," said the Sage, "I heard many reports
  That Guinness brought rest to the brain,
Since when, if depressed or a bit out of sorts,
  I've drunk it again and again."

"Yes, I see," said the youth, "but there's one other thing
  In which I am most interested.
You've consumed a repast rich enough for a king;
  Pray, how d'you contrive to digest it?"

"In my youth," said his father, "the Guinness I drank
  Kept me free from interior strife;
And the fitness for which I've got Guinness to thank
  Has lasted the rest of my life."

GUINNESS
IS GOOD FOR YOU

G.E.250.D.

Above: **Press advertisement by Gilroy (1931).**

Opposite page (clockwise): **A new version of Lewis Carroll's emblematic poem 'The Mouse's Tale' (1934). Decoration from press advertisement 'Thirst Move' (1934). The first colour advertisement for Guinness to appear in a newspaper;** *Daily Express,* **28 June 1933.**

A TALE of TWO GLASSES

("It's a long tail," said Alice, "and quite pointed.")

Jimmy said to a pal
That he met in the
Mall, "What d'you
say to a drink? It's
too soon for a
feed. But the posters
say GUINNESS
will put some
strength in us;
so GUINNESS,
I think, is just
what we need."
"Delighted, old
boy, I will join
you with joy,"
said his friend,
nothing loath,
"if you'll pay
for the two."
"Very well,"
replied J.,
"since you
put it
that way,
I will
pay for
them
both
And I'll
drink
them
both
too."

(With apologies to the Author and Printers of "Alice in Wonderland.")

G.E 184 A

DAILY EXPRESS .... JUNE 28th.

'Tis the Voice of the Lobster,

I heard him declare,
"I am ready for dinner, if Guinness is there."
As a duck demands peas, so a lobster appeals
For a Guinness at dinner and other such meals.
It brings out the flavour, the epicures say,
(And who should know more about flavour
than they?)
A lobster's a good thing, but do not forget a
Lobster with Guinness is twenty times better.

GUINNESS
and LOBSTER

Right: **Alice and the White Knight hunt the Loch Ness Monster, from a press advertisement in January 1934.**
Below: **London Underground poster (1931).**

was so well received that a second edition was hurriedly printed.

In 1934, Guinness used Alice and the White Knight to comment on the frenzied spate of monster-spotting that was going on at Loch Ness. Throughout the autumn and winter of 1933, numerous sightings of 'Nessie' were reported, climaxing in December with some enigmatic film footage of the elusive creature. A couple of weeks later, in January 1934, Alice took a trip to Monsterland. The White Knight took the precaution of equipping himself with a lobster-pot.

'"What is the lobster-pot for?" Alice asked in a tone of great curiosity.

"Well," said the White Knight, "it's an invention of my own. I'm going to look for this Monster, you see, and it might come in handy."

"It's not very likely the Monster would turn out to be a Lobster," said Alice.

"Not very likely, perhaps," said the Knight, "but it's as well to be prepared for *everything*. That's why I'm carrying this Guinness – nothing like Guinness with Lobster, you know. And there's another reason."

"What is that?" asked Alice.

"Well, something tells me I'm going to need a Guinness," said the Knight. "The Monster might put up a resistance – and who can resist a Guinness? You see, I'm

A
Sane Lunch Party
(Many Guinness Times removed from Lewis Carroll)

"If you knew Time as well as I do," said the Hatter, "you'd only have to whisper a hint to him, and round goes the clock in a twinkling! One o'clock–

GUINNESS TIME

('I only wish it was,' the March Hare said to itself in a whisper, 'I'm simply longing for a Guinness')

very determined. In fact, either I shall capture this Monster or else –"

"Or else what?" said Alice, for the Knight had made a sudden pause.

"Or else I shan't, you know," said the White Knight.'

Alice's popularity in Guinness advertising remained undiminished until the Second World War, and two more Alician titles appeared among the annually-produced 'Doctor's Books': *Jabberwocky Re-versed*, illustrated by Gilroy, and *Alice Aforethought*, with illustrations by Antony Groves-Raines.

In the starkly progressive post-war years, however, the denizens of Wonderland and Looking-Glass World seemed somewhat out of place, and were gradually phased out. Not, however, before they had a chance to join in

the celebrations marking an amalgamation between Guinness and the confectionery firm of Callard & Bowser: the Walrus talked of 'hops-and-crops and Butter-Scotch and what is Good for You' and there was yet another parody of 'Jabberwocky', titled 'Almalgawocky'.

The Alice characters had a nostalgic revival during the Festival of Britain, and were part of the Guinness 'Festival' clock. The following year, 1952, saw the publication of the fourth collection of Guinness carrolls, *Alice, Where Art Thou?* illustrated by Antony Groves-Raines in a fantastical *trompe-l'oeil* style.

The last Carrollian Guinness book, *Alice Versary*, appeared in their bi-centenary year, 1959, after which the campaign was abandoned. In 1965, however, Guinness took space in *The Times* to commemorate the one

Covers from two of the Guinness Christmas books: (*left*) *Jabberwocky Re-Versed* **(1935) illustrated by John Gilroy, and** (*above*) *Alice Aforethought* **(1938) designed by Antony Groves-Raines.**

"There ought to be a book written about me, that there ought! And when I grow up, I'll write one... but then," thought Alice, "shall I never get any older than I am now?"

Confectionately yours

Alice could not help pointing her finger at Tweedledum and saying, "First Brother!"

"Nohow!" Tweedledum cried out briskly.

"Next Brother!" said Alice, passing on to Tweedledee. But he only shouted out "Contrariwise!"

"Look before you leap to conclusions," said Tweedledum. "Just because we're alike ..."

"We might be no more alike," broke in Tweedledee, "than a glass of Guinness and a packet of Butter-Scotch—and *still* belong to the same family."

"But," began Alice, "Guinness is brewed—"

"Exactly," said Tweedledee, "Guinness's brood includes Callard. And Bowser, of course."

"By adoption, you know," said Tweedledum gravely.

"But Guinness is tall, rich and handsome," Alice ventured to object.

"Callard and Bowser sweets are small, rich and toothsome," said Tweedledum. "There's a strong likeness, if you look."

"Goodness!" said Alice.

"Precisely," said Tweedledee.

Issued jointly by

GUINNESS and CALLARD & BOWSER

Guinness, brewers of stout since 1759, seven years ago acquired control of Callard & Bowser, makers of fine Butter-Scotch and other confectionery since 1837.

ALICE never did get any older but the book about her *was* written, and that has reached a ripe old age.

Exactly 100 years ago tomorrow the real Alice received from Lewis Carroll her copy of the *Adventures in Wonderland* which had just been published. That gift was also a gift to the parodist.

The parodies that *Alice* inspired were of a new sort—they were apologetic, kindly and always complimentary to the author.

Among the many who were glad to owe a debt to Lewis Carroll was Guinness. In the 1930's a series of *Alice* parodies appeared which were so well received that two books of them are preserved in the British Museum Library.

Guinness and *Alice* have since gone their separate ways; we at Guinness look back on those days with affection, and we remember this anniversary with gratitude and respect.

hundredth anniversary of the publication of *Alice's Adventures in Wonderland*, and to express their gratitude for the help given to Guinness by Lewis Carroll and his dream child.

With the Alice advertisements, Guinness once again set a precedent, and many other advertisers have subsequently looked to Alice and her friends to help them sell anything and everything, from teabags and biscuits to photocopiers and laxatives!

Other literary parodies were, in the main, of nursery rhymes, popular ballads and the like, although some classic poetry – including Shakespeare – was used to turn a Guinness joke. One advertisement, for example, showed a glass of stout and asked 'Can I compare thee to a summer's day?', while another showed a

bottle of Guinness and an empty glass and asked: 'When shall we three meet again?'

Richard Barham (who, as Thomas Ingoldsby Esq., wrote *The Ingoldsby Legends*), W. S. Gilbert, Thomas Hood and the author of *Struwwelpeter* all provided material for excellently worked verse parodies, such as the story of Tim Tonks 'a puny lad' who, despite his 'sighs' could not increase his 'size'. Inspired by Thomas Hood's brilliant punning style, the ballad tells how Tim falls in love with Betsy Brown: 'a buxom lass and tall; but though he thought her simply great, she made him feel quite small'. Then, seeing a poster which advertised 'Guinness for Strength', Tim takes a Guinness-a-day, with the result that he soon becomes 'twice the man he was before' and wins Betsy's admiration – and love! And so,

Above left: **A suitably nonsensical press advertisement from 1958, celebrating the seventh anniversary of Guinness having acquired control of Callard and Bowser!**
Above right: **Advertisement from *The Times*, 3 July 1965.**

social and romantic success were added to the already preposterous claims made for Guinness:

Thus happy Tim gained Betsy's hand
And two feet in addition.
By drinking Guinness he attained
The height of his ambition.

This and other verses were collected and published as *The Guinness Legends*, the second Christmas book for doctors, in 1934.

Although many of these parodies were skilful and amusing, and always contained plenty of references to Guinness, some were precious and self-indulgent. 'What did Wordsworth say in 1802?' asked one advertisement, '"Milton thou shouldst be living at this hour" – it's Guinness Time!' Painfully esoteric, such advertising was too clever by far, and no doubt confused – perhaps even alienated – a good many drinkers.

In contrast, Guinness made liberal use of more prosaic material such as nursery rhymes ('Sing a song of Guinness a bottle full of good'), children's games ('One, two, this'll do; Three, four, to restore'), music-hall songs ('Where did you get that head, where did you get that smile?') and monologues ('"The boy stood on the burning deck" – the audience had fled – have a glass of Guinness when you're tired!').

One of the most popular of these advertisements was a rhyme that survived changing times and styles and was still being used in

Illustration by Antony Groves-Raines from the 1952 Guinness Christmas book, *Alice, Where Art Thou?*

Daisy, Daisy

(To the tune of "Daisy, Daisy"))

Daisy. Daisy, give me a sandwich, do!
Don't be lazy, give me my Guinness, too!
For lunch isn't lunch without it,
So hurry up about it!
It's nice to drink
And it's nice to think
That a Guinness is good for you!

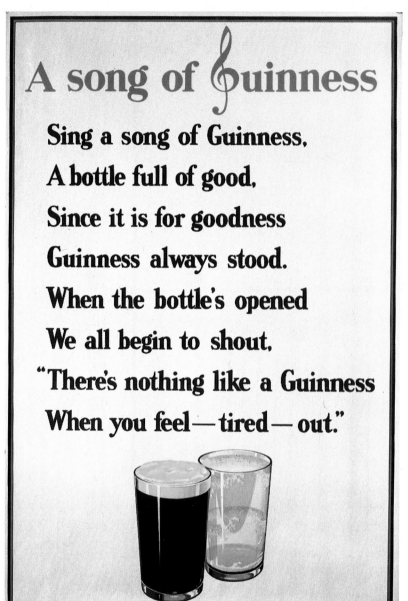

Under the spreading chestnut-tree
A glass of Guinness stood.
The smith, a mightier man is he—
His Guinness did him good.
And would it do the same for me?
My Guinness, yes it would!

Opposite: **Cover and illustration from** *Songs of Our Grandfathers*, **the 1936 Guinness Christmas book, decorated by Rex Whistler.**

press adverts and on off-licence show-cards as late as the fifties:

> My Mother said that
> I never should
> Miss my GUINNESS –
> *As if I would!*

Victorian popular songs – which still had a currency in the thirties – inspired the 1936 Guinness Christmas Book, *Songs of our Grandfathers.*

Illustrated with wit and charm by Rex Whistler, *Songs of our Grandfathers* recalled a lost era. Within three years the safe, secure Victorian age was to seem impossibly remote as Britain was catapulted into a world war that claimed – among so much else – the life of the delicately whimsical Mr Whistler.

In 1938, a new dance called 'The Spreading Chestnut Tree' was all the rage, and Guinness quickly cashed in with posters and advertisements carrying a parody of Longfellow's famous poem about the village blacksmith.

Comic ballads, light verse, popular songs, rhymes and stories – they have all been used to find different ways of expressing the same thing – that Guinness is good-humoured as well as good for you.

'My heart leaps up when I behold a Guinness in a glass,' said one advertisement, and then added 'But what are Wordsworth without a Guinness?' The question, of course, was purely rhetorical.

If he can say as you can
Guinness is good for you
How grand to be a Toucan
Just think what Toucan do

GUINNESS
BEHIND BARS

When, in 1979, a toucan who made television commercials for Guinness opened the door to his cage and, quite literally, flew the coop, it made headline news in all the popular dailies: 'HELP! HE'S TOUCAN OFF – Big Flap as Bird in Advert Escapes.' It was a dramatic chapter in the twilight years of one of the best-loved characters in British advertising.

He began his career forty-four years earlier, in 1935 – as a pelican! John Gilroy had devised an idea on the 'Guinness-a-day' theme – it showed a pelican with seven pints of Guinness balanced on its beak, and for copy carried the old rhyme:

A wonderful bird is the pelican,
Its bill can hold more than its belly can.
It can hold in its beak
Enough for a week:
I simply don't know how the hell he can.

Dorothy L. Sayers was asked to provide some rather less offensive copy; instead, she changed the bird into a toucan, reduced the number of glasses from seven to two and wrote an apposite little rhyme (opposite).

Which is how the toucan was hatched. It took a little while for his character to fully develop, and over the next few years he underwent a subtle transformation – putting on a few pounds in weight and having cosmetic surgery on his over-long beak. He went on to weather all the ups and downs of the next four decades of Guinness advertising, was retired in the sixties, brought out of retirement ten years later, and only finally pensioned off in 1982.

Although the toucan became and remained the central character in the Guinness menagerie that grew up over the following years, he was not, in fact, its founding member. That honour goes to the sea lion, who had first run off with the zoo-keeper's Guinness a few months earlier.

Gilroy had visited Bertram Mills' Circus at Olympia, and while he was watching a performing sea lion doing balancing tricks, it occurred to him that the animal was probably smart enough to balance a glass of Guinness on its nose. It was an idea that would inspire one of advertising's longest running – and most delightful – campaigns. The slogan: 'My Goodness – My GUINNESS' which, with and without the animals, was used for years, was a masterstroke of punning invention; 'My Goodness' serving both as a reference to the drink – Guinness is good for you – and as an exclamation of astonishment.

The sea lion went on to serve his country (and his keeper) during the war, and he reappeared again in the fifties, on one poster watching with astonishment as the keeper (now a circus-trainer) practised his old balancing trick.

The Guinness animals provided a solution to a difficult problem which Bensons were facing with Guinness advertising. They had begun work on a campaign featuring a human 'Guinness Family', but couldn't agree among themselves how it should be done. Gilroy recalls that 'Everyone who was involved in deciding on the posters hated someone in the

Below: **Gilroy's runaway sea lion made his debut on a poster in the summer of 1935.**
Right: **This seasonal variation on the sea lion joke was made by Gilroy for a Christmas card containing a recipe for Guinness-strengthened Christmas pudding!**
Below right: **The sea lion and keeper reverse roles in this 1958 poster by 'Wilk'.**

Guinness Family – for being too handsome or too ugly.' The idea of using animals to advertise Guinness provided an alternative approach that no one could object to. The only human present in this series was the anxious little zoo-keeper, who was a caricature of Gilroy himself.

The animals, with their strongly-defined personalities, caught the public's eye and imagination, while their simple antics were quickly and easily understood: Guinness was good enough to steal – if, that is, you happened to be an amoral creature such as a sea lion or an ostrich.

The ostrich (overleaf) first appeared in 1936, a distant cousin probably of the one who had featured in a press advertisement two years earlier: 'Even when an ostrich buries its head in the sand, you still know it is an ostrich and nothing else. Even if someone were to give you a Guinness, having first removed the distinctive creamy head, you would still know it was a Guinness.'

The ostrich on Gilroy's 1936 poster didn't have its head in the sand, but it did have a Guinness in the neck – and still in the glass!

The ostrich poster brought a flood of letters from members of the public who thought Gilroy had drawn the glass the wrong way up. It was not, of course, a mistake. Gilroy knew that if the poster's scenario was to make sense, the silhouette of the glass had to look like a glass. One of his preliminary sketches for the poster shows, alongside life studies of ostriches, two necks: one with an upright glass in it, the other with an inverted glass. The upside-down glass might, logically, have been correct, but in the drawing it looks more as if the bird has

Right: **An advertisement in Latin, from** *The Times,* **2 July 1936. As here, no translation was thought necessary!**

Lines Suggested

to a *Claſſical Scholar*

by some recent

GUINNESS Advertisements

THE CRANE AND THE STORK

Si tibi, Grus, esset, longove Ciconia collo,
Qui sapor in nostris faucibus esse solet:
Si mihi combibulum tibi fata, Ciconia, guttur,
Si mihi donassent congrua colla Grui:
Vos sapidos, longos equidem deducere potus
Possemus pulsis sollicitudinibus.

THE GIRAFFE

Aspice dum monstrum! quanti dispendia colli!
Si mihi dent haustus sex bona fata pedes!

W.H.D.R.

GUINNESS PRODEST—*PROSIT*!

Far right: **Magazine advertisement by Lobban (1952).**

The Ostrich, travellers recall,
Enjoys his Guinness, glass and all.
How sad the Guinness takes so long
To get to where it makes him strong!

Right: **Unused poster design by Gilroy, and (*below*) the giraffe's only other appearance on the sides of London buses during 1957.**

Opposite: **Gilroy's ostrich poster (1936).**

swallowed a weight from a set of scales, which is doubtless why it was crossed through by the artist.

It was thought, however, that the enquirers deserved a rather more inventive explanation. 'I replied,' says Gilroy, 'that the ostrich had been imitating the sea-lion by balancing the glass on his nose. It had then flicked it up into the air, opened its beak, and the glass had gone down the easiest way – to be properly enjoyed in its stomach.'

In fact, it seems never to have got as far as the stomach. Every subsequent appearance of the bird shows the glass still firmly wedged in its neck – unless it kept swallowing glasses, just to see what two (or more) could do!

The controversy and the ostrich were kept alive, and twenty years later a comic verse was specially composed on the subject:

The Truth about
THE OSTRICH

The Ostrich, many people think,
Has never learned the way to drink:
They say the goblet, glass or cup
Is going down the wrong way up,
And Guinness that you cannot taste
Is so much Guinness gone to waste.

Perhaps these carpers never knew
The truth about the Ostrich, who
Enjoys, as every child can tell,
His Guinness and its glass as well.
And Guinness answers that old question –
What gives the bird his strong digestion.

In 1936, a press advertisement introduced a giraffe to the zoo:

A Toucan of Affection

For fifty years, the toucan was part of the Guinness corporate image. Here are a few of the many appearances he has made in Guinness advertising over the years.

GUINNESS
–HIM STRONG

See what Big Chief Toucan do

GUINNESS GOOD FOR PALEFACE

Above left and right: **Show-cards for off-licences (1954 and 1960).**
Right: **Press advertisement (1951).**
Below right: **Pottery lamp-base and part of a cruet featuring the toucan, together with one of a set of three flying toucan wall-plaques (1957).**
Below left: **Poster (1982).**

Goodness-on-sea

Going for a pint as good as Guinness?

The upper half of the Giraffe
to him is just a Waste.
But how sublime if GUINNESS TIME
gave us six feet of Taste!

This same joke appeared in a somewhat esoteric guise when, on 2 July 1936, *The Times* contained what must be the only beer advertisement to be printed in Latin!

Gilroy produced a number of sketches for poster-designs featuring the giraffe, but his only other appearance was as an advertisement on the side of buses in 1957.

In the autumn of 1936, the tortoise crept onto the hoardings for the first time as an appropriate illustration of the 'when you're tired' slogan; and the following year the tortoise was among the animals that were seen entering the Ark in the only Guinness advertisement to ever use a Biblical theme.

Right: **The Guinnesses went in two-by-two in this 1937 press advertisement.**
Below right: **The pelican makes a belated poster appearance in 1939.**
Below left: **Gilroy's tired tortoise crept on to the posters in 1936.**

but
there's nothing like
a Guinness

Have a
GUINNESS
when you're **TIRED**

My Goodness
My
GUINNESS

As the New Gnu knew
very soon at the Zoo
Guinness is good for you

My Goodness
my GUINEAS

TAX DODGERS

FINANCE BILL

My Goodness
MY
VODKA

Above left: **1940 saw the arrival of a 'gnew' Guinness character.**
Above: **Strube parodies Gilroy in the** *Daily Express,* **19 May 1939.**
Left: **Illingworth in the** *Daily Mail,* **23 October 1958.**
Below: **Strube in the** *Daily Express,* **12 June 1935.**

My Goodness

MILK
MARKETING
BOARD

MY BUSINESS

Opposite: **After years of chasing animals, the keeper finds one is chasing him! Poster by Gilroy (1939).**

Gilroy's animals had been a fairly docile bunch, but in 1937, he showed the keeper being chased by a lion. It was, perhaps, a surprising choice, since most people feel rather less at ease with a lion than, say, a *sea* lion! Of course, Gilroy did give him a twinkling eye and a genial smile that helped to belie his carnivorous tendencies, but the public never really took him to their hearts.

Although the pelican had originally been rejected in favour of the toucan, he eventually waddled onto a poster in 1939 (with a week's Guinness in his bill). Another late arrival was the 'new gnu' who appeared in several coloured press advertisements, but who was never given full poster status – despite his irresistibly soulful expression.

The Guinness animals were quickly ensconced as part of popular British culture, and like all establishment figures they soon found themselves being used by Fleet Street's cartoonists. Strube was first, with a cartoon in the *Daily Express*, that reflected Beaverbrook's opposition to the Milk Marketing Board which had been set up two years earlier and which was about to hold a referendum to decide whether the nation's farmers wanted it to continue.

Over twenty years later, the joke was still being used by cartoonists: In 1958, for example, Illingworth employed the sea lion to comment on Russian premier Khrushchev's clamp-down on drinking in the USSR.

Strube parodied the pelican poster in 1939 with a caricature of Viscount Simon, then Chancellor of the Exchequer, defeating the tax-dodgers.

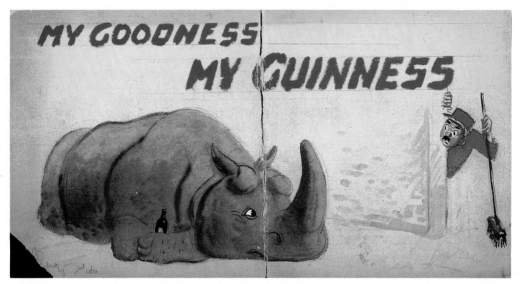

Other Guinness animals were to follow during the war, and into the fifties – most notably the crocodile, the kangaroo and the kinkajou – but Gilroy sketched a great many other birds and beasts that were never finally exhibited. These included a bull, a beaver, a woodpecker, a rhinoceros, a cockatoo, a donkey, a cobra, an elephant, an octopus and a team of racing greyhounds.

There were good reasons why some of these birds and animals never worked for Guinness – the woodpecker, perhaps, because of its association with cider and the elephant because it was the trade mark of the Fremlin brewery. The cobra was doubtless considered too scary and the greyhounds might have been thought to have implied that Guinness condoned gambling. Why, however, the rhino and the hippo were not used remains a mystery – particularly since they could have proved a popular asset to the advertising zoo.

Once again, Guinness were instrumental in starting a trend in advertising, and since the founding of the Guinness zoo, many other

John Gilroy drew all his Guinness animals from life. Here are some of the many studies he made at the Zoological Gardens in Regent's Park, London.

Gilroy's Zoo

My Goodness
My GUINNESS

"My Goodness—My Guinness"

G.E.1189.A

companies have enlisted the aid of all creatures great and small to sell tea and paint, petrol and breakfast cereal.

Although 'My Goodness My Guinness' became primarily associated with the animals, Guinness used it for other situations in which a Guinness drinker might be alarmed to find his Guinness under threat, as in Bateman's illustration of a juggler who mixes up his Indian-clubs with someone's bottle of Guinness.

Back in 1938, Gilroy used the slogan to accompany his first 'workman' poster in two years. Once again the cartoonists dashed off parodies, among them the indefatigable Strube, Bert Thomas and the *Sunday Pictorial*'s Tac, whose cartoon featured the man who was about to change the course of European history – Adolf Hitler.

The events that were shortly to ensue, would also change the course and style of Guinness advertising.

Opposite: **Magazine advertisement by H. M. Bateman (1941).**
Right: **Gilroy's poster (1938) which inspired a cartoon** (*below*) **by 'Tac' in the** *Sunday Pictorial*, **30 April 1939.**

My Goodness My GUINNESS

My Goodness Mein KAMPF

GUINNESS
AS USUAL

GUINNESS
IS GOOD FOR YOU

9

WHAT THE SITUATION DEMANDS

On Saturday, 2 September 1939, life in Britain went on much as usual. Arsenal football team, then top of the First Division, beat Sunderland five goals to two, tennis at Budleigh Salterton was rained off, and in the *Daily Express* Rupert Bear was having an exciting new adventure with a sea serpent.

Rowntree's Fruit Gums cost twopence a tube and Player's Navy Cut cigarettes were one shilling and a halfpenny for twenty. You could rent a brand new radio for just one shilling and nine pence a week, and a bottle of Guinness required the staggering capital outlay of seven pence in old currency.

The next day the world turned upside-down. At 11.15 on Sunday morning, 3 September, people anxiously gathered around wireless sets over the length and breadth of the country. The BBC's announcer introduced the Prime Minister, Neville Chamberlain.

'I am speaking to you,' he began in a solemn, weary voice, 'from the Cabinet Room at 10 Downing Street. This morning the British Ambassador in Berlin handed the German Government a final Note stating that unless we heard from them by eleven o'clock that they were prepared to withdraw their troops from Poland a state of war would exist between us.'

Millions of listeners – in London flats, country cottages, suburban villas and industrial back-to-backs – held their breath. 'I have to tell you that no such undertaking has been received, and that consequently this country is at war with Germany.'

The broadcast was scarcely over when the unearthly cry of the air-raid sirens wailed out for the first time, heralding six years of turmoil and anguish, rationing, conscription, bombing, evacuation, separation and loss.

But somehow the people of Britain managed to put a brave face on things. There were the movies – Bette Davis in *The Little Foxes*, Orson Welles in *Citizen Kane*, Garland and Rooney in *Babes on Broadway*, Greer Garson in *Mrs Miniver* and Charlie Chaplin in *The Great Dictator*. Hollywood catered for all emotional requirements – the humour of Bob and Bing, the romances of Fred and Ginger and the pathos of Dumbo and Bambi.

On the wireless there was Mr Tommy Handley and his ITMA gang, Arthur Askey and Dickie Murdoch, Elsie and Doris Waters, Dick Barton – Special Agent, and of course Miss Vera Lynn. In the newspapers there were the daily antics of Little Nipper, Useless Eustace and that saucy young lady – Jane.

And then there was Guinness. Good old Guinness! Ever ready with a smile and a joke to encourage spirit-raising as well as Guinness-downing!

Most advertisers, however, found very little to smile about with numerous Government restrictions on their activities constantly coming into force. Catalogues, brochures and promotional circulations were banned, and Christmas 1939 saw the appearance of the last 'Doctor's Book' to be produced by Guinness for several years: *Prodigies & Prodigals*.

Among the moral and improving tales was an apposite story about St John Flint who, unlike his valorous ancestors, preferred cello playing to feats of arms. Until, that is, he discovered Guinness:

> A daily Guinness strengthened him
> And much improved his figure;
> It filled our hero to the brim
> With energy and vigour.
> His Guinness-given manly strength
> Enabled him to carve a
> Career, and to achieve at length
> Renown at Balaclava.

A more familiar character, the long-

Opposite: **Window display (1941).**
Right: **The keeper and the sea lion 'join up'! Poster by Gilroy (1940).**
Overleaf: **Guinness going over the top in another of Gilroy's war-time posters (1940).**

My Goo
My

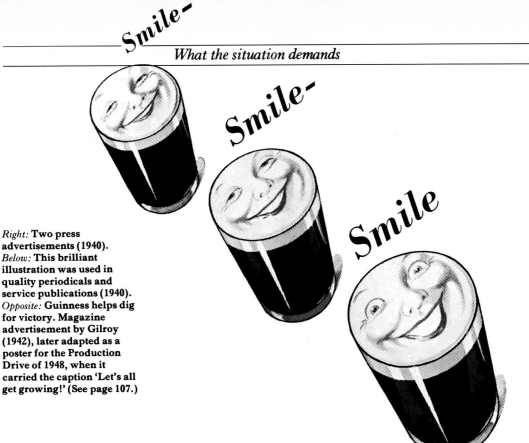

Smile—
Smile—
Smile

To Women
who have to work hard

$\left(\begin{array}{c}\text{AND THAT MEANS}\\ \text{EVERY WOMAN NOW}\end{array}\right)$

TODAY—more than ever—what you need is Guinness. Guinness for strength through a hard day's work. Guinness for calm nerves. Guinness for a cheerful outlook. Thousands of women are finding the new strength they need in a glass of Guinness every day. Prove for yourself that "Guinness is good for you."

Right: **Two press advertisements (1940).**
Below: **This brilliant illustration was used in quality periodicals and service publications (1940).**
Opposite: **Guinness helps dig for victory. Magazine advertisement by Gilroy (1942), later adapted as a poster for the Production Drive of 1948, when it carried the caption 'Let's all get growing!' (See page 107.)**

suffering zoo-keeper, joined the Home Guard and so won the admiration of the sea lion that instead of stealing the keeper's Guinness, it went so far as to deliver it to him on a salver. The sea lion was also to be seen delivering barrels of Guinness to the hard-working ENSA troupes.

The keeper was promoted to sergeant for another advertisement, and he supervised a practice-session in Molotov-cocktail throwing – with alarming consequences.

A Government Order, issued in May 1940, imposed restrictions on the use of new paper for posters larger than 60in × 40in. As a result, the last regular Guinness poster change went onto the hoardings that autumn with the slogan, 'Thousands are finding strength in Guinness'.

In the summer of 1941, Guinness began printing on the reverse of old poster stocks. The design – simply the old 'Guinness is Good for You' slogan – had to have as dark a background as possible in order to minimise the amount of 'show-through' from the other side. The results were rather more functional than artistic.

Although no new posters appeared until the end of the war, stocks of old designs were used to keep a Guinness presence on the billboards of Britain, and on the walls of London's underground stations.

In the press Guinness remained prolific advertisers, despite the restrictions on advertising space imposed by another Government regulation in March 1942.

Within a month of the outbreak of war, advertisements with a topical message had

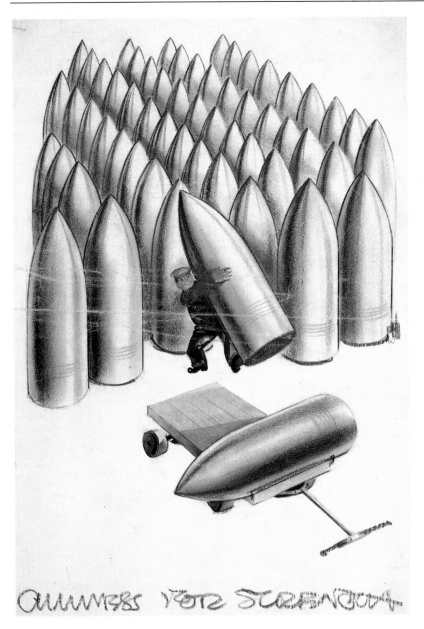

This page: **Some of Gilroy's unused war-time ideas.** *Opposite:* **Old jokes revived for the illustrated press, by** (*clockwise*) **H. M. Bateman (1944); John Gilroy (1941); Bateman (1943); Gilroy (1942).**

begun to appear: 'What's the use of worrying?' asked one, 'Troubles pack up and go when Guinness appears'.

Both the smiling Guinness-glass and the smiling clockface were a cheery sight in the gloom-filled columns of the daily press; or peering through the taped-up windows of pubs and off-licences.

Not too surprisingly, the Benson copywriters were quick to promote the idea that such critical times called for an increase in Guinness consumption. '*Today* – more than ever – what you need is a Guinness', and once again, medical testimonials were produced in order to bring home the full force of their argument: '"In times of nervous strain, Guinness accomplishes marvels" – says a Doctor.'

With so many men away in the forces, a specific campaign was directed towards the women they'd left behind them – Guinness was good for 'women who have to work hard (and that means every woman now)'. One advertisement went so far as to make the outrageous claim that 'Guinness has saved many a poor woman's life'.

In a more humorous vein, 'Guinness for Strength' provided John Gilroy with a number of new situations for his strong-men, including a gardener whose efforts were inspired by the government's 'Dig for Victory' campaign; and, in one of Gilroy's many unused designs, a sailor loading shells single-handed – after a Guinness, of course!

Guinness played its part in keeping up the morale of the forces by placing many lighthearted advertisements in the service publications. One showed a sailor having 'Guinness is good for you' tattooed on his chest; another showed a billet of sleeping troops (with an empty Guinness bottle at the foot of every bed) blissfully unaware of their bellowing sergeant-major.

A popular advertisement featured a soldier and a sailor enjoying a glass of Guinness and a game of draughts. 'I have Guinness for strength,' says the soldier, 'that's strategy!' 'I have it on you,' replies the sailor, 'that's tactics!'

At one time, during the early days of the war, Gilroy contemplated enlisting the support of the nation's leaders. One idea he produced was a sketch of Churchill and Chamberlain shaking hands and remarking that what was needed was more Guinness; and he even thought of using Churchill's well-known bulldog image, and having the pugnacious canine

'...nine hundred and ninety-two, nine hundred and ninety-three, nine hundred and ninety-four, nine hundred and ninety-five, nine hundred and ninety-six, nine hundred and ninety-seven...'

HAVE A GLASS OF GUINNESS WHEN YOU'RE TIRED!

My Goodness — My GUINNESS

"I feel like a GUINNESS!"
"I wish you were!"

"My Goodness — My Guinness"

G.E.1130

103

My Goodness—
My GUINNESS

Guinness for Strength

run off with Herr Hitler's Guinness!

Gilroy also devised a number of other variations on the old 'My goodness – my Guinness!' theme which showed Guinness drinkers having their goodness threatened by a variety of wartime perils: it was dive-bombed by a Spitfire, launched with a torpedo and spirited away by gremlins.

Not only do old slogans never die, they seldom fade away! 'Have a glass of Guinness when you're tired', and 'I feel like a Guinness! – I wish you were!' found themselves conscripted into service.

On the day that war was declared, the zoos of Britain destroyed all poisonous snakes, reptiles, rodents and insects in case they were accidentally liberated by a falling bomb. Most other species, however, remained on show – even in London's Regent's Park, which was badly blitzed on several occasions. These creatures' stoicism was shared by the inmates

of the Guinness zoo whose antics continued to feature in advertisements. Gilroy even succeeded in exhibiting one or two new animals to the public, among them a brown bear, a pair of walruses and an absent-minded mother kangaroo.

In addition to all the familiar themes and jokes which were reworked for war-time advertising, Guinness also produced a number of original and inventive ideas, of which one of the best was 'What the Situation Demands' with its wheel (for putting shoulder to), socks (for pulling up), brass tacks (for getting down to), etc.

F. C. Harrison's collection of visual puns neatly summarizes what Guinness and their advertisers were doing from 1939 to 1945 – looking always on the bright side, they made a generous contribution towards helping a war-weary public cope with what the situation demanded.

Above left: **The kangaroo joined the Guinness zoo with this 1942 press advertisement. Gilroy adapted his design for a poster in 1947.**
Above right: **Press advertisement (1944).**
Opposite: **F. C. Harrison's classic 1942 advertisement; an idea which Guinness reworked several times (see page 19).**

WHAT THE SITUATION DEMANDS

Painted by
F. C. Harrison

1. WHEEL *for putting shoulder to*

2. SOCKS *for pulling up*

3. STONE *for not leaving unturned*

4. BRASS TACKS *for getting down to*

5. TRUMP CARD *for playing*

6. BOLD FACE *for putting on it*

7. BELT *for tightening*

8. GUINNESS *for strength*

GUINNESS
FOR STRENGTH

10
LET'S ALL GET GROWING

'This is IT – and we are all going nuts!' wrote a *Daily Mirror* reporter on the eve of V-E Day, 7 May 1945. 'There are thousands of us in Piccadilly Circus. We are dancing the conga, the jig and "Knees-up, Mother Brown", and we are singing and whistling and blowing paper trumpets.' Germany had unconditionally surrendered after five years, eight months and four days of war.

But it was to be three more months before V-J (Victory Japan) Day on 15 August marked the end of all hostilities; and it was to be many years before Britain shook itself free from the post-war slump.

Guinness was making life brighter a few days after war ended with the appearance of a new member of the Gilroy zoo. Following the example of his forbears, he filched the keeper's Guinness which doubtless explains his contented smile (overleaf).

At Bensons, the end of the war brought with it a number of changes. William Knight (who had been chairman since 1931) was succeeded by Norman Moore, Sidney Irwin was the new art director and Bobby Bevan became managing director. Bevan, who has been described by one of his colleagues as a great man with a keen brain and a powerful intellect, began moulding Guinness advertising into the shape that was to make it, during the fifties, the most stylish and prolific advertising of its day.

The first new Guinness poster to be displayed for several years went on to the hoardings in November 1945 and featured the familiar smiling glass and a combination of equally familiar slogans. One variation depicted the last words of a Guinness, 'Don't look now, but I think we're about to be swallowed'. Although many people found the idea amusing, there were others who thought Guinness were going just a little too far in trying to anthropomorphise the pint.

The smiling glass became ubiquitous. As part of a post-war export drive, it did a balancing act on top of the earth demonstrating how 'Guinness Invigorates the World'. Its photogenic features were to be seen, in a film premiere programme, as a 'Coming Soon' poster in a cinema foyer, and in another advertisement its portrait in an elegant gold frame was exhibited in an art gallery. That picture was after one of the classical Old Masters (*c* 1933) but a rather more modern perspective was taken in an oil painting by Erichobbsky, executed in the style of Georges Braques or Pablo Picasso.

'Erichobbsky' was the thinly disguised signature of the young artist Eric ('Bruce') Hobbs, who joined Bensons in 1946 and four years later succeeded Sidney Irwin as the agency's art director. It says something, perhaps, about modern art that when Hobbs (who had painted the picture at home over the weekend), inadvertently left it on a train, he was able to knock off a copy in just ten minutes.

My Goodness

Let's all get growing!

Opposite: **This poster by Gilroy (1949) is the artist's personal favourite.**
Left: **A reprise for the Guinness gardener (1948).**
Right: **Advertisement for *The Cherwell* and *The Isis*, illustrated by Bruce Hobbs (1948).**

This is nothing like a Guinness
BUT THEN THERE *IS* NOTHING LIKE A GUINNESS

Among the new generation of copywriters were Stanley Penn, who had joined Bensons in the late 1930s and returned there after serving with the RAF during the war, and John Trench who became a member of the agency's staff in 1946, after a distinguished army career. Between them, these two men were to be responsible for the majority of the Guinness copy that was to appear over the next twenty years. They followed in the footsteps of Ronald Barton and Bobby Bevan as masters of pun, parody and pastiche.

For example, a drawing of a ghostly Elizabethan man giving a glass of Guinness to his own decapitated head was accompanied by the following rewrite of a famous Stanley Holloway monologue:

> 'I'm a bodiless Inn-spectre,' he remarks with ghoulish glee,
> 'But anything I lack *de corps* I make up in *esprit*.
> For there's Body in a Guinness, and it puts new life in me
> When its Head's tucked underneath my arm.'

Guinness advertising was often smart, sometimes sly but always single-minded, although both Penn and Trench tended to be modestly dismissive of their work. 'Guinness advertising at this time,' says John Trench 'was an exercise in intense over-indulgence by a group of over-educated men.' It was rumoured that Guinness advertising was written by black men from Balliol! Trench, in fact, studied at the Royal Military Academy, but as far as his colleagues at Bensons were concerned he was always regarded as an 'Honorary Balliol Black'. One thing he and Penn were particularly good at was thinking-up games, puzzles and diversions on which to hang, coincidentally, an advertisement for Guinness. The earliest of these entertainments invited readers to see how many words they could make from the one word GUINNESS – there are, incidentally, over forty.

The copywriters' wit and invention during this period – however close it came to self-indulgence – has never been surpassed. Nor has the golden age of illustration which began in the immediate post-war years and lasted for a decade or more.

The infrequency of posters in the immediate post-war period meant that Gilroy art was less often seen on hoardings. Nevertheless, the kangaroo made his poster appearance in 1947 and, two years later, Gilroy designed one of his most popular – and his own personal favourite

My Goodness— My GUINNESS

TRY THIS – IT'S GOOD!

Gaze fixedly at a point midway between the man and the glass of Guinness. Then move the picture close to your face, and the man will appear to drink the Guinness. After that, go and have one yourself . . .

Opposite clockwise: **Gilroy press advertisement (1949); a Guinness illusion (1947); a variant on the famous 'Willow Pattern' plate, by Antony Groves-Raines (1947).**
This page clockwise: **Two press advertisements promoting productivity (1948); two 'Guinness for Strength' designs by Gilroy (1948); original artwork (dissected for printing) for Gilroy poster (1947).**

My Goodness

— there's stacks to be done on the land!

My Goodness

we've got to

get weaving to balance

our export trade!

Pennmanship

'Stanley Penn,' wrote Charles Hennessy, remembering his days at S. H. Benson, 'was a tall, slim, slightly stooping, almost foppish figure, with drooping hands and long, flat, out-turned feet. His hair was gingery-brown, thin and straight and his eyes protruded slightly, like those of Eddie Cantor from under sleepy Max Beerbohm lids. His face had acquired in middle-age Audenesque lines, like a parched river-bed. He kept his face straight until he told a joke, when it would fold, using its whole network of lines into the triumphant and faintly self-approving beam of the born funny man.'

Millions grow to appreciate the Goodness of **GUINNESS**

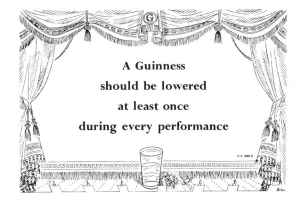

A Guinness
should be lowered
at least once
during every performance

With a flower in his buttonhole and wearing a pair of carpet slippers, Penn gave a mildly eccentric atmosphere to the clubbish copy department at Bensons. Over the years he produced not only a great many verses, but also an endless stream of little jokes and ideas that frequently provided Guinness with some of its finest miscellaneous advertisements. Many of these were included in *A Little Judicious Levity*, a celebration of his Pennmanship, produced by Bensons to mark his retirement in 1966. He died in 1984, aged 83.

Life is brighter after Guinness

Bottle and Jug

(A passage which, by some oversight, Lewis Carroll never wrote.)

"Hatta's only just out of prison," said Haigha.

"What was he in for?" Alice ventured to ask.

"A month," said the King.

"I mean," said Alice patiently, "what crime had he committed?"

"He's going to take someone else's Guinness," replied the King nervously.

"But does he go to prison *before* he takes the Guinness?" asked Alice.

"Of course," said the King. "That's how we

do it in Looking-Glass Land. It's much better that way. Then when he does take it no-one will mind."

"Except me," said Haigha, stretching out his hand, just too late. "Will you have the goodness to return my Guinness," he cried to Hatta.

"I can't have the Goodness if I return the Guinness," said Hatta. "My Goodness, your Guinness," he added politely.

(By arrangement with Maravilas & Co. Ltd.)

GUINNESS IS GOOD FOR YOU

Advertisement by Antony Groves-Raines for *The Illustrated London News* **(1954).**

– 'Guinness for Strength' poster. It showed a farmer, quite literally, putting the cart before the horse (see p. 106).

Gilroy had first submitted the idea years before but had been told that it 'wasn't Guinnessy enough'. When it did appear it was everywhere applauded. The artist himself received a standing ovation on walking into the Garrick Club.

'When I drew this poster for Guinness,' says Gilroy, 'it drew a testimonial from an unexpected source. The late Sir Alfred James Munnings RA, is reputed to have said "I'm supposed to be a great painter of horses. Another man, greater than I can make horses happy and lovable, while mine are powerful and polished. I would love to see that man – Gilroy's – horses hanging in the Royal Academy".'

Gilroy's carthorse never did reach the Academy, but he did something even more

important by enlivening the roadside hoardings of Britain. The farmer, like the zoo-keeper, is Gilroy and, according to the artist, the horse's benign expression bears a striking resemblance to that of his father.

A subsequent advertisement explained why it was that the farmer was between the shafts. Coming to a toll-bridge where horse-drawn vehicles were charged a one shilling toll while *hand*-drawn vehicles were free, he simply put the horse in the cart and pulled it himself, thereby saving one shilling and demonstrating just how strengthening Guinness can be.

Alice and friends were back again, this time in a new series of literary advertisements by John Trench and Antony Groves-Raines, for inclusion in high-quality periodicals such as the *Illustrated London News*, *Country Life*, *The Field* and *The Tatler*.

At the other end of the social scale, a number of the Guinness characters were enlisted to support the Government's National Production Drives, which were aimed at getting Britain out of its post-war depression. Although this was an altruistic gesture by Guinness, and although the posters and press advertisements never mentioned the product, the iconography that was employed left no one in doubt as to who was responsible for them.

One of these advertisements carried the following verse:

'Production,' said the Toucan,
'Is simply up to you, so work
As hard as you can
And do what two can do.'

It had been a tough, exhausting and often depressing ten years since war had been declared. But with the dawn of a new decade in view there were expectations of renewed prosperity and opportunity just around the corner. As a beacon of hope, on 2 April 1949, the lights of London flashed into life after ten years of darkness and in Piccadilly Circus the Guinness clock told Guinness time once again. It heralded the festivities of the fifties.

Trenchant Wit

'John Trench,' recalled Charles Hennessy, 'had a kindly face with a high-brow's high brow and hair that had never really taken. His eyes were flat-based half-moons, like Mr Chad's, with Malteser pupils and laugh lines at the outer corners. It was a face more apt for smiling than for frowning.'

In addition to advertising copy, John Trench wrote several thrillers — *Docken Dead*, *Dishonoured Bones* and *What Rough Beast* — and was a highly accomplished writer of light verse. He was undoubtedly Benson's finest verse writer and he had the curious distinction of being probably the only person to have a piece of advertising copy included in an anthology of poetry, when his poem about 'The Sensible Sea-Lion' appeared in Penguin's *More Comic and Curious Verse*.

FROM THE GUINNESS VARIETY PROGRAMME

The Sensible Sea-Lion

The sea-lion, naturalists disclose,
Can balance balls upon his nose,
And some, so neatly does he judge it,
Ask, " If a ball, why not a budget ? "

No head for figures is his knob—
His eye's not on the Chancellor's job.
He doesn't balance gains with losses,
But pleasure on his own proboscis.

And rightly, he prefers to win his
Spurs by demonstrating Guinness.
Perhaps this very session he'll
Be chosen as Lord Privy Seal.

LIFE IS BRIGHTER AFTER GUINNESS

BUILD THE MAN UP

Oh once I was weak, bullies, once I was small,
 (Weigh, Heigh, blow the man down)
Me arms was like matchsticks, I'd no strength at all
 (Oh give a slight puff to blow the man down).

Me chest it was hollow, me knees used to knock,
 (Weigh, Heigh, knock the man down)
One morning off Brest I was rove through a block
 (Oh give us a feather to knock the man down).

To look at me now, boys, would anyone think
 (Weigh, Heigh, rub the man down)
When the mate cried Belay ! I was blown in the drink
 (Oh give us a towel to rub the man down).

Now from Hamburg to 'Frisco I'm famous for brawn,
 (Weigh, Heigh, build the man up)
I've a voice to out-bellow a gale off Cape Horn
 (Oh give us a Guinness to build the man up).

It was Guinness what done it, let no one forget,
 (Weigh, Heigh, give the men strength)
Now I'm mate of this hooker I'll see that you get
 A Guinness a day just to give the men strength.

G.E.2078.E

Besides their conventional advertising overseas, Guinness have seized a great many unconventional opportunities to promote themselves in foreign climes . . .

My dear Sirs,
Here is Jose Francisco Rego writing to you these few lines again, hoping that they will go and find you all my dear unknown friends in good health.

This letter, from the Azores, was one of a great many that were sent from around the world to Mr A. W. Fawcett, managing director of Guinness Exports in Liverpool, in 1953.

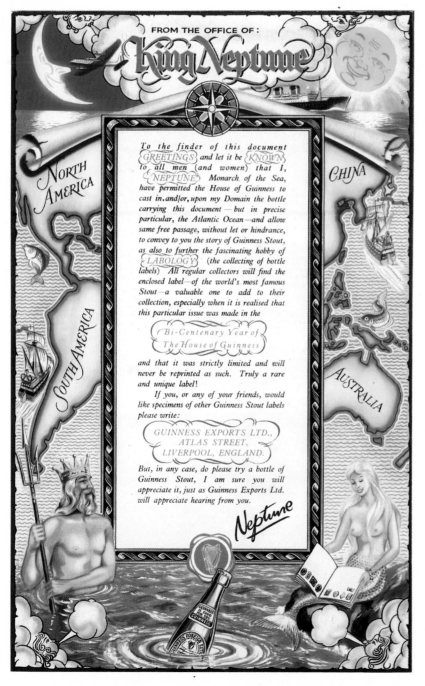

A dynamic, somewhat tyrannical man, Arthur William Fawcett, was known as *The Guinness Exporter*. For years, he had been managing director of Macfee's, the Guinness-owned bottling and exporting company in Liverpool, and had a reputation as an eccentric, colourful character and a uniquely gifted salesman. In 1950, Guinness Exports was established, and Fawcett came out of semi-retirement to be its managing director. By 1962, he had increased overseas sales of the Dublin-brewed Foreign Extra Stout sixfold.

The letter from Jose Rego was in response to one of Fawcett's extraordinary public relations stunts. In 1954, a large number of Guinness bottles were dropped in the Atlantic, Pacific and Indian Oceans, each containing a parchment greeting with a tear-off form for the finder to reply, with details of where and when the bottle had been found.

The replies (which are still being received, thirty years later) came from such exotic places as the Bahamas, Tahiti and Mexico, from where a gentleman wrote to say that he had found his bottle while 'at work, stone-breaking at the edge of the beach in the prison where I unfortunately find myself at the moment'. He went on to ask if Guinness could 'very kindly be good enough to help me within the limit of possibilities'. Unfortunately, it is not known what reply he received.

The headmaster of a school on Elenthera, in the Bahamas, had a more modest request, 'Do you throw any full bottles overboard?' A 14-year-old Eskimo boy found one of the bottles in 1962, while on his first Polar bear hunt in Ungava Bay, Canada. And another reply came from a gentleman who had found his bottle in the Gladstone Graving Dock – in Liverpool!

Among Fawcett's other inventive ideas were leprechaun charms and miniature Guinness bottles, but, in 1958, he embarked on what was probably his wildest scheme ever. Learning that Liverpool Corporation was about to scrap the city's gas lamps, Fawcett purchased them for £3 each. In an advertisement in *The Liverpool Echo*, Guinness Exports offered a free lamp to any Liverpudlian overseas who could suggest ways to increase the export of Guinness. As a result, Liverpool gas lamps are now to be found outside a bank in Washington and in the garden of the editor of Australia's *Picture Post*.

Every one of Fawcett's seemingly crazy campaigns, however, had its purpose. As one of his young assistants, later chairman of Guinness Exports, Eric Beedell, recalls Fawcett had a clear strategy in mind all the time; it was this: 'Find your prospective Guinness drinker. Tell him Guinness is good for him. And everything else will follow as a simple matter of course.'

GUINNESS
for strength

PRINTED IN GREAT BRITAIN BY JOHN WADDINGTON LTD. LEEDS

11

FIFTIES FRIVOLITIES

There was an unmistakable air of frivolity in Britain as the new decade dawned and brought with it hopes of a brighter tomorrow. It was a mood which the creative staff at S. H. Benson were quick to grasp. A new Gilroy poster appeared on the hoardings, showing a jovial sun beaming down on the smiling Guinness glass.

This was Gilroy's last poster as a staff member at Bensons. After twenty years of being the chief artist of Guinness Advertising, Gilroy decided to go freelance. As a result, posters by other artists began to appear. The first of these was by 'Wilk' (Dick Wilkinson), who illustrated a new interpretation of the 'Guinness for Strength' theme, with a workman lifting a manhole cover with a steamroller on top.

The idea was devised by John Trench, who is justifiably proud of this, his only poster idea – and, in particular, of the '123HUP' registration number. The bulk and the weight of the steamroller and the sheer muscular force with

Opposite: **Poster by 'Wilk' (1951).**
Right: **Poster by Edward Ardizzone (1954).**

which the workman blithely lifts the manhole cover, make Wilk's design the most powerful of the post-girder Strength advertisements.

An altogether less satisfactory interpretation, showing a removal man shifting a piano, appeared several years later from a new contributor to Guinness Advertising, the illustrator Edward Ardizzone. Although Ardizzone produced a set of delightful illustrations to the Guinness booklet, *Game Pie*, his style wasn't nearly strong enough to work successfully as a poster.

Christmas 1950 saw the reappearance of the annual Guinness book for doctors. Entitled *A Guinness Sportfolio*, it took the form of a sporting almanac with verses by Penn and Trench and decorations by Groves-Raines.

The mood was still curiously Victorian, as was that of the following year's book, *Album Victorianum*, which looked back a hundred years to the Great Exhibition of 1851. The illustrations were by Ronald Ferns, Eric Fraser and Benson's new art director, Bruce Hobbs.

The Great Exhibition was also the original motivation behind that euphoric, national jamboree, the Festival of Britain. Thought up during the last year of the war and begun in 1947, when it looked as if Britain were about to pull out of its post-war slump, the Festival proved something of an anachronism with money and building materials being made available for a fun fair at Battersea and a vast complex of futuristic structures on the South Bank, at a time when many people were still without a home. Built by a Labour Government, the Festival became a target of the Conservative opposition, headed by Winston Churchill and Lord Beaverbrook. However, the popular response to the Festival was very different; it was warmly received and, from the day it opened, on 3 May 1951, there were long queues of enthusiastic visitors who eagerly seized an opportunity to escape their dreary daily grind and marvel at the wondrous images of a brave new world.

The Festival of Britain was described as 'A Tonic to the Nation', so that it was appropriate that Guinness – who had for so long been a tonic to the nation – should be associated with the project.

Since all the nation knew about 'Guinness time', what could be better than a special Guinness clock? In fact, a Guinness *Festival* clock. Designed by Messrs Lewitt-Him and made by Baume and Company Limited of Hatton Garden, the clock was a fantastically whimsical affair and, therefore, a highly suitable timepiece for the Festival Pleasure Gardens at Battersea Park, with its tree-walk and its Emett Railway.

Every fifteen minutes, the eccentric little building burst into life: the sun spun round; the keeper rose from under an umbrella

The Senior Angler shook his head,
" There is no catch in it," he said ;
" You cannot say a story's tall
" If you can nail it to the wall."

This trophy proves that he's not bluffing —
The proof of the fish is in the stuffing.
But why the Guinness, you'll be thinking ?
The proof of the strength is in the drinking.

Illustrations by Antony Groves-Raines from (*this page***)** *A Guinness Sportfolio* **(1950), (***opposite***)** *What Will They Think of Next?* **(1954) and** *My Goodness! My Gilbert and Sullivan!* **(1961).**

ringing a bell; the ostrich emerged from a chimney; marionettes revolved on a whirligig; the Mad Hatter came out of his house and fished up a diminishing string of fishes from a pond; and, finally, the doors opened to reveal a pair of toucans pecking at a Guinness Time Tree hung about with watches.

The clock was an enormous success and one of the most popular attractions at the Festival Gardens, where it became a mecca for the nursemaids of London and their charges. It would be interesting to know how many subsequent Guinness drinkers gained their first, affectionate opinion of Guinness from sitting in their prams and push-chairs around that Festival clock.

For several years after the Festival, Guinness clocks, with slight alterations, toured the seaside resorts of Britain, delighting young and old alike – including the present writer,

A Groves-Raines Portfolio

Despite being one of the most technically accomplished illustrators of his day, Antony Groves-Raines is now largely forgotten and his work generally unknown. He illustrated eight of the Guinness Christmas booklets and several series of coloured press advertisements. His other work included illustrated books for children and a set of richly elegant decorations for a collection of carols entitled *On Christmas Day in the Morning*.

Groves-Raines's early work comprised delicate line illustrations reminiscent of Rex Whistler, but his style later matured and developed into richly detailed pictures that stand as classic examples of *trompe-l'oeil* art. In order to achieve this astonishing three-dimensional quality to his work, Groves-Raines first created plasticine models of every scene to be depicted, using real flowers, properties and drapes. The process was time-consuming. 'Roughly speaking,' Groves-Raines once wrote, 'I plunge into the job like a woodworm into a very thick, dark beam, emerging

months later, limp and exhausted on the other side. And as I emerge, I am never wholly without the suspicion that I have, in fact, bored through the entire length of the beam from end to end with a happy knack of turning what might be simple and easy into the elaborate, difficult and disagreeable.'

It was a process not usually associated with the production of advertising art, and one which led to un-met deadlines and, for the art director at the advertising agency, a number of sleepless nights.

At the end of his labours, the artist was invariably dissatisfied with the result: 'When at last all the drawings are completed I am naïvely astonished that such infinite pains should produce such very meagre results.' But Antony Groves-Raines's illustrations remain among the rarest and finest gems in the treasury of Guinness advertising.

Above: **Illustration by Bruce Hobbs from** *Album Victorianum* **(1951).**
Above right: **Poster advertising the Guinness clock (1951), for overprinting with venue.**
Right: **Guinness time in Piccadilly Circus.**
Far right: **Poster, by Ray Tooby, advertising the special Festival Guinness brewed in 1951.**

who used to sprint the length of Margate Prom (as fast as his little legs would carry him) several times a day to watch the clock perform.

The Festival clock also influenced the shape of Guinness clocks to come – the illuminated timepiece in Piccadilly Circus was first modified to show a pair of sea lions juggling with the keeper's Guinness, and then built in the shape of a cuckoo clock with a toucan instead of a cuckoo.

A Festival poster, drawn by *Eric Fraser*, featured Alice and her chums on the South Bank – Father William balanced the Skylon on the end of his nose; a glass poured Guinness on the Tweedle Brothers from the top of the Shot Tower and the Dome of Discovery became the smiling Guinness face. To commemorate the Festival, Guinness also produced a special brew and a poster advertising it by Ray Tooby.

Guinness and Alice go to the Festival of Britain. Poster by Eric Fraser (1951).

GUINNESS
IN FESTIVAL LAND

"What a lot there is to see!" Alice exclaimed.

"That's why it's called the South Bank Sight," said the Hatter. "Now let's hear you re-cite."
So Alice folded her hands and began:–

"He thought he saw a Dome that held
Discoveries galore;
He looked again and saw it was
A Guinness by Thames shore.
'We know it's Good for You,' he said,
'Need man discover more?'"

(With acknowledgements to Macmillan & Co. Ltd.)

GUINNESS IS GOOD FOR YOU

Gardener's
GUINNESS

which is Particularly Enjoyable

These two posters represent something of a crossroads in Guinness advertising: the Fraser design recalling the intricate artwork and elaborate copy of the past, and the Tooby poster foreshadowing the simpler, 'modern' style that, within a decade, would typify Guinness advertising.

For some while, however, continued use was made of the old tried and trusted ideas and slogans, like 'Have a Guinness when you're tired' or 'A Guinness a day' with its variation 'Had your Guinness today?' And in the press, a series of daily advertisements, illustrated by Wilk, exploited this theme. For example, Monday's Guinness gave you a good start, Tuesday's kept you up to the mark, and Thursday's put new life into you.

FRIDAY'S GUINNESS

The week is very nearly through –
Come on! One extra spurt will do!
You're braced in every nerve and sinew
When you have Guinness Goodness in
   you.

Further variations were introduced for special days: Boat Race Day ('helps one stay on course'), Grand National ('it spurs you on over and over again'), Guy Fawkes Day ('makes things go with a bang') and Christmas ('full of good cheer').

This was only one of several long-running series which, during the fifties, attempted to give far greater cohesion to Guinness's press advertising. One series, illustrated in a sprightly style by Victoria, featured verse conversations (to the metre of Lewis Carroll's 'Will you walk a little faster') with actors, porters, airmen,

'It doesn't matter where you are'

...the Skipper said to me

" A Guinness always buoys you up on life's
                        tempestuous sea.
From Kirkwall round to Plymouth, by paddle, sail or screw,
It looks the same, it tastes the same,
                        it's just as good for you.
So will you, won't you join me,
                        and have a Guinness, too ? "

GUINNESS IS GOOD FOR YOU

Above left: **Gardener's Guinness:**
'Weekends bring you lots to do –
How it takes it out of you!
When you're tired of spades and rakes,
Guinness gives you What it Takes.'
Press advertisement (1953).
Above right: **Advertisement for the Ulster Grand Prix programme (1953).**
Left: **Press advertisement by 'Victoria' (1953).**

Opposite page: **Press advertisement (1952).**
Centre: **Guinness presents the London Zoo with two toucans (1950).**
Right: **The Guinness menagerie 'adopted unanimally' in 1949:**
'All the Guinness animals That everybody knew,
The toucan and the pelican, The seal and kangaroo ...
You saw them on the posters, The lion and ostrich, too.
Well, Guinness have adopted them
You'll see them in the Zoo.

" You ought
to know
by now . . .

Nothing but
a Guinness

*is good enough
for me* "

You get to know, after a while, if a drink is really doing you good.

Guinness not only has a clean satisfying taste, a taste that never cloys — it's a grand *smooth* drink; and it gives you an unmistakable feeling of well-being too.

No wonder millions of glasses are drunk every day, by people who want real value for their money.

Bill
and
Coo!

TOCO-TOUCANS
Presented to the Zoo by
Messrs. Arthur Guinness Son & Co. Ltd., 1950

sailors, tourists and couriers, all of whom assured the reader that it didn't matter where you were – you could always enjoy a Guinness.

There were also plenty more imaginative ideas from Stanley Penn and John Trench, such as a punning line for a theatre programme – 'Overture and Be-Guinness please', and an advertisement in the *Police Review* showing an empty glass and a page from a notebook carrying the words: 'Taken down in evidence.'

These advertisements invariably hit the mark, whether simple quips – 'Guinness is good at Thirst Aid' – or cunning parodies: 'The curfew tolls the knell of parting day, the lowing herd winds slowly o'er the lea, the ploughman homeward plods his weary way, ah! that's when I find Guinness good for me.'

During the 1950s, 'real people' began, for the first time, to feature in Guinness advertisements – although their early appearances were frankly rather gauche.

The language was frightfully clean and terribly middle-class: 'Guinness Time! There's welcome words! The very sound of them's enough to give you an appetite. Guinness is just the job with food because of its clean, bracing taste. It makes you feel chirpier from the very first sip!'

This development, however, was revolutionary. Since the idea of depicting Guinness drinkers had been abandoned in the thirties, the only people who had ever been seen drinking it were cartoon animals and labourers. In the press, although not on the posters, all that was changing, and Guinness drinkers were depicted as being young, smart, healthy and successful – in fact, the model fifties consumer image.

In the 1970s, Guinness advertising campaigns to women became legendary; what is not so widely known is that Guinness began seriously directing advertisements at women as early as 1950, using sketchy illustrations and a gossipy style that suited the columns of *Woman's Weekly* and *Woman and Home*. 'We'd been married for 21 hours 15½ minutes' began one ad. The speaker and her husband are due to board the 11.24 to Casablanca (where else?)

Christmas Number
1949

In 1946 the first issue appeared of *Guinness Time*, a house magazine for the Park Royal Brewery. This entertaining and informative periodical was issued quarterly, later half-yearly, until its demise in 1975.

Many of the *Guinness Time* covers, of which these are examples, were specially designed by artists who worked on Guinness advertising. The copies shown here had covers illustrated by (*top*) John Gilroy and (*bottom*) André Amstutz.

The Best of Times

when her husband orders her a Guinness in the airport lounge.

'Darling, whatever made you order Guinness for me? I've never had it before!' James tries to look serious. 'You've never flown before, either. Two exciting things in one day!'

Saucy fellow! Anyway, James's little woman soon gets outside a Guinness, and finds the 'cool, clean, *unsweet* flavour – *Heavenly*!'

Advertising during the post-war years began to move more and more away from commercial art and towards the use of photography. One of the earliest uses of a photograph in an advertisement was a rather dull picture of a swaying field of barley, used in the mid-forties. But the advertisements which most benefited from the development of photography in advertising were those featuring food, and it became no longer necessary for one of the Benson draughtsmen to have to paint lobsters and oysters or, indeed, glasses of Guinness.

Despite these hints of things to come, much of Guinness advertising remained centred on the familiar animal characters. In 1949, Guinness participated in an adopt-an-animal scheme run by the London Zoo, sponsoring the upkeep of those animals particularly associated with Guinness advertising – the

lion, kangaroo, ostrich, pelican, toucan and sea lion. The following year Guinness presented two toucans to the Zoo – and both events were commemorated by advertisements.

Novelty glass cloths (Guaranteed All Linen Fast-Colours) were produced, featuring Gilroy's toucan and kangaroo posters (five shillings, including Purchase Tax), and, on the posters, the toucan made a come-back, deftly using his long beak as a bottle-opener to demonstrate that 'Opening Time is Guinness Time'. He next went on to feature on two other Guinness posters that introduced the 'Lovely Day for a Guinness' slogan – on one, he doubled as a weathercock; on the other, he (and some of his friends) put on a stunning formation-flying display.

A year or two earlier, a new animal had been added to the Guinness menagerie. His curious habit of hanging upside down caused the keeper to bend over backwards to get a view of what was happening and several members of the public to wonder whether the poster had been pasted on to the hoarding the wrong way up.

Some of these enquirers were, in fact, not mistaken since at least one bill-poster managed to get the keeper rather than the kinkajou

Posters by Gilroy: 1952 (*below*), **1954** (*right*) **and 1955** (*overleaf*).

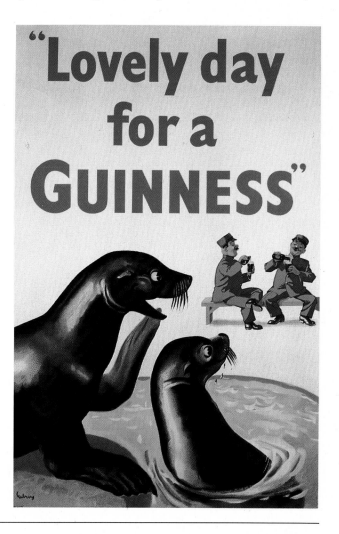

upside down! Although the kinkajou was never as fondly regarded as some of the Guinness animals, and although the tag-line 'Think what kink-ajou can do' was a feeble parody of the toucan poster, the little creature worked effectively to get Guinness noticed and the inverted lettering caught the eye of millions of people during the summer of 1952.

The kinkajou was too recent an addition to the Guinness family to feature on the next pictorial poster which went on to the hoardings the following summer. It celebrated the Coronation of Queen Elizabeth II on 2 June 1953, and it was the first British poster to have neither copy nor any reference to the advertiser or his product.

Drawn by Gilroy, the idea for the poster (with its subtle reminder of Guinness's strengthening qualities) had come from Stanley Penn, who later wrote 'I always thought the idea for that poster was the apogee of my career as a copywriter because, although I enjoyed thinking up ideas, I found writing copy very hard work.'

The public was charmed by the poster, and it is said that this affectionate display of loyalty by the Guinness animals was much appreciated by Britain's young queen.

Two years later, in 1955, Guinness produced another striking poster, this time to coincide with the General Election. It simply said: 'DOWN WITH GUINNESS! – then you'll feel better.' Again, it was designed by Penn and had been printed several months before the Election was announced. It was held in store until a date had been set for polling day and then it was quickly despatched to bill-posters all over the country.

The poster was about to go onto the hoard-

ings when it occurred to someone that they ought to check in case there actually was a candidate named Guinness. As it happened, a member of the Guinness family, Chips Channon, was standing in Southend, so care had to be taken to ensure that the poster was not displayed anywhere within that constituency.

Although these posters were important fore-runners of the many inventive topical advertisements that were to follow, it was an insignificant press advertisement at the time that spoke more prophetically of the future course of Guinness advertising. It showed a couple enjoying a Guinness as part of a TV snack.

The televising of the Queen's Coronation incontrovertibly established television as the communications medium of the future. The emergence of commercial TV also established it as the market-place of the future.

The caption-less Guinness Coronation poster (*top*) devised by Stanley Penn and drawn by John Gilroy (May–July 1953), and a press advertisement from 1955, the year Guinness went into television advertising.

Just for the Record

paedias could resolve. Sir Hugh decided that a book ought to be written, listing the longest, shortest, tallest, and fastest things in the world. Such a book, he decided, would provide an excellent gift for members of the licensed trade – enabling them to settle the kinds of disputes that often arise between drinkers during bar conversation. Sir Hugh took up this idea with an under-brewer at Park Royal, called Christopher Chataway (who was himself a record-breaker for 3 miles and 5000 metres) and he arranged for Ross and Norris McWhirter, a pair of twins who had been collecting superlative data for several years, to have lunch with Sir Hugh at Park Royal Brewery in September 1954.

As a result of their meeting – and much subsequent research – the first *Guinness Book of Records* was published in 1955. It was an instantaneous success, and, within three years, had sold 430 000 copies.

Following Ross McWhirter's death, Norris has continued to edit the book, and has become a nationally known personality. Now published in 23 languages, the total number of books sold in all editions uniquely passed 50 million copies in 1984. If the annual British sales alone were piled on top of each other, they would make a column roughly twice the height of Mount Everest which is a fairly superlative effort.

Guinness Superlatives, who publish the *Guinness Book of Records*, also produce a wide range of reference books. These include titles on pop music (such as the best selling *Guinness Book of British Hit Singles*), sport (Athletics, Cricket, Golf, Rugby, Soccer and Tennis which are an established Facts and Feats series), entertainment (Film, TV and Theatre) and also general works such as the *Guinness Book of Winners & Champions*, the *Guinness Book of Answers* – and the book you are now holding in your hand!

Strictly, of course, *The Guinness Book of Records* is not an advertisement but, since some four million copies a year are sold throughout the world, bearing the famous name, it is not a bad form of public relations.

The book came about as a result of a seemingly trivial event in the early 1950s. Sir Hugh Beaver, then managing director of Guinness, was out with a shooting party in Ireland and badly (and for him rarely) missed a bird. The bird's speed led to a discussion about which game bird flew the fastest, a question which no amount of burrowing in encyclo-

Guinness Books – a wide-range of specialist subjects for would-be Masterminds (and another way of advertising the Guinness name).

My Goodness-
a 200th birthday label !

BREWED IN LONDON & DUBLIN BY ARTHUR GUINNESS SON & CO.

1759 **1959**

GUINNESS
EXTRA STOUT
BOTTLED BY
BREWERS & BOTTLERS
EVERYWHERE
DUBLIN AND LONDON

Gilroy

GA/PI/2400

12

GUINNESS POSTERS COME TO LIFE

On the evening of Thursday, 22 September 1955, an estimated two million people – chiefly in the London area – were watching the opening night of commercial television. It was not without its problems, one of which was that the advertisements popped up in the middle of programmes without any warning. For example, a boxing match was being televised and the commentator had just remarked: 'Now the other boy's nose is bleeding too!' when suddenly the Guinness zoo-keeper appeared shouting 'My Goodness'. This remark, however, was not intended as a comment on the state of the boxer's nose, but was due to the fact that he had just spotted the sea lion waddling off with a glass of Guinness on *its* nose. Guinness television advertising had arrived. Arriving had not been particularly easy.

Lord Moyne, vice chairman of the Guinness Board, had written to *The Times* on 31 July 1953, to say that he considered the BBC network 'entirely adequate and commercial TV an unnecessary and extravagant extension which the snowball effect of competition would oblige all advertisers to use if once it were open'.

His fears were understandable. As he explained to a reporter on the *Sunday Graphic* in November 1953: 'If we have commercial TV and our competitors – or the soft drink concerns – started advertising, we'd have to consider doing the same. This might force us to raise our prices or reduce our profits.'

When, the following year, the TV Bill had its reading in the House of Lords, Moyne voted against it and during the debate vehemently expressed the hope that 'the commercial circus would never be put on the air'.

The next day, Bobby Bevan resolutely told a Guinness meeting at Bensons: 'It is the policy of this House to support commercial television.' Guinness raised no protest.

An important change in the way Guinness viewed its advertising had already taken place. From 1929, advertising manager, Martin Pick, had been answerable not to the main Guinness Board, but to a 'brewer in charge of advertising'. It later became clear that advertising was of such vital importance to the company that Pick was made responsible to trade director, W. E. Phillips.

This was the position when, in 1955, Pick retired and was succeeded by T. L. (Tommy) Marks. Marks was a man with a strong artistic taste and he knew and mixed with many artists. He was personally responsible for Guinness using the work of Abram Games, John Nash and Edward Ardizzone.

Marks was in total agreement with Bobby Bevan. Guinness needed to advertise on television just as much as it needed to advertise on the poster hoardings almost thirty years before. Although the cost of advertising was high (then £1000 a minute), the potential audience was enormous.

The only problem was to know how to use effectively this new advertising medium. Not unnaturally, Bensons looked first to the Company's advertising heritage. Gilroy's famous posters had always proved popular, perhaps a way could be found to bring them to life on television. Which is exactly what they attempted to do, actually calling their advertisements 'A Guinness Poster Comes to Life'.

The first commercial was a life-action film based on the sea lion poster and featuring Charlie Naughton from The Crazy Gang and a temperamental, second-hand German sea lion which would only respond to German words of command.

The result was quaint and curious but scarcely brilliant, and it is probably as well that Guinness lost the draw that was made to decide whose advertisement would be the very first to be screened (an honour that went to SR Toothpaste).

For the time being, Bensons wisely abandoned further attempts to recreate posters in live action, and turned instead to animation and the studio of Halas and Batchelor. A year earlier, in 1954, John Halas and his wife Joy Batchelor had achieved a huge success with their animated film of George Orwell's *Animal Farm* (one of the few feature-length animated films to have been produced at that time outside the Walt Disney Studio). During the next five years they were to produce some of the finest animated advertisements of the day including films for Daz, Rael Brook shirts and Murraymints.

Opposite: **The Gilroy animals greet the appearance of a new label celebrating 200 years of Guinness (1959).**
Right: **Charlie Naughton and friend in the first Guinness television commercial (1955).**

The subject for the Halas and Batchelor Guinness advertisements was still the old posters, but they were now brought to life in the simple, stylised method of animation, pioneered by the American UPA Studio in the early fifties.

The sharply contemporary style of animation and the lively, tuneful jingles did much to ensure the popular reception of these advertisements. The basic idea, however, was so derivative it severely weakened the commercials' impact. Later, after a return to live action (including a cyclists' picnic with a toe-curling rendition of 'Daisy, Daisy, give me a sandwich do!'), Halas and Batchelor produced some snappy little scenarios for a series called 'The Prompted Animals'. The pelican, kangaroo, ostrich and toucan appeared on screen to talk about the goodness of Guinness. The words, however, were put into their mouth by the off-screen prompter as they were either too shy to speak, or – in the case of the pelican – had a bill full of Guinness.

The ostrich, who was rather less reticent, gave a particularly delightful performance:

NARRATOR: The Guinness ostrich speaks.

OSTRICH: Guinness gicks gou gup gen goure gired.

NARRATOR: Is that Ostrich talk for Guinness picks you up when you're tired?

OSTRICH: Ges.

NARRATOR: Then for Guinness's sake speak English.

OSTRICH: Guinness gives gou grength.

(Kicks sand at screen and buries head.)

NARRATOR: Certainly Guinness gives you strength, but if you take your neck out of the sand we might understand you.

(Pop!)

No wonder you're swallowing your words!

OSTRICH: Guinness gis good gor gou.

NARRATOR: And *that* means – Guinness is good for you.

OSTRICH: Gulp!

When Bensons next returned to live action they had adopted a more serious approach, deciding to show people instead of animals. Although the results were often unintention-

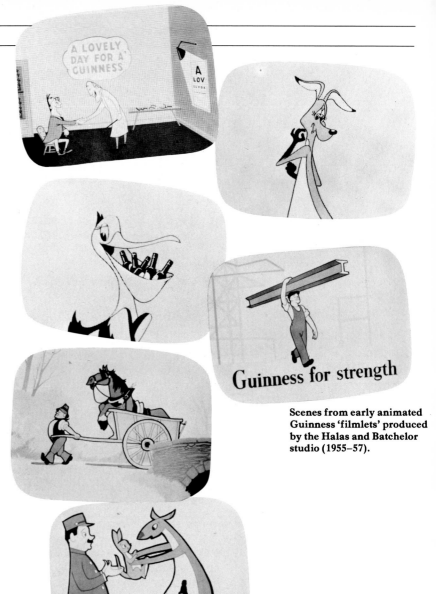

Scenes from early animated Guinness 'filmlets' produced by the Halas and Batchelor studio (1955–57).

The Guinness barman pouring a drink for one of the 'chaps from the factory down the road' (1958).

Above: **Scenes from Guinness Tango Time, another Halas and Batchelor commercial (1957).**
Right: **The sponge-rubber Guinness head that winked at viewers at the end of each commercial.**

advising you to keep Guinness at room temperature in winter, keeping it cool in summer ('My Missus says I fuss too much, but I believe in keeping it out of the heat of the day'), and telling you how Guinness is brewed ('They take some of the – er – brewing barley – look, I've got some here!'). He also began the long-running campaign using the slogan '5 Million Glasses are Enjoyed Every Day'. And for those who found his accent too Kensington-and-Chelsea, he was dubbed with a Yorkshire brogue for northern screening.

That the TV campaign shuttled back and forth between live action and animation was an indication of the fact that Bensons had yet to come properly to terms with what could and what could not be achieved on the small screen. The clearest example of this was Bobby Bevan's attempt to recreate on television the famous smiling-glass. At considerable expense, a foam replica of the face used on the posters was created and actually made to wink. For some while this gruesome device was used as a signature to all Guinness TV commercials. As one retired Guinness executive says: 'Television should have been used to show Guinness as it is, in its beautiful reality, not as a glass with a winking rubber sponge on top!'

It wasn't long before cartoon animation was being used again – this time with a superbly drawn series showing Guinness animals engaging in a variety of popular dances. Ostriches did the tango, toucans the samba, turtles the cha-cha and sea lions the soft-shoe shuffle to the accompaniment of a song, the predominant lyric of which was 'Guinness is good for you' (or, in the film about the ostrich, for 'gou'). In addition to the well-known creatures, the series also included the contemporary idea of a band of cats playing skiffle.

Among the voices used in this series was that of Jon Pertwee who was one of a distinguished group of actors and comedians including Spike Milligan, Peter Sellers, Kenneth Connor, Richard Hearn (Mr Pastry), Gordon Jackson and Jeremy Hawk. Messrs Hawk and Pertwee

ally funny, it should be remembered that Bensons had had very little experience in selling Guinness, as it were, straight.

The chief protagonist in these early commercials was a barman with a remarkably refined accent: 'Usual Sir? I thought so – there's nothing like a Guinness after a tiring day. The chaps from the factory down the road like to drop in for a Guinness when they knock off. Wonderful how it bucks you up when you're tired. Cheers you up just to look at it.'

Another commercial introduced the idea of Guinness's compatibility with food: 'Though I say it myself we do serve good food here and my customers like something good to go with it – a glass of Guinness. We serve a tremendous lot of it here especially with snacks,' [pronounced 'snecks']. 'There! Isn't that a picture? Well, I'll be taking it over to the Lady and Gent. I reckon they know what's good for them.'

The barman made several appearances –

also featured in a series of cinema commercials about crazy inventions such as a rocket-powered bicycle and a heli-hat. Although none of these contraptions worked, in each case the inventor, after a Guinness, was able to do whatever he was trying to do – but without his machine! A number of animated 'Guinness Filmlets' were also screened in cinemas, including an oculist whose eye-chart spells out A – LOV – ELYDA – YFORAGUI – NNESS...

Animated TV commercials were once again given up in favour of another attempt at realism. This time the target audience was women, and the results were hilarious. A series of middle-class young ladies try their first Guinness and tell their clean-cut, pipe-smoking, tweed-jacketed menfolk what they think of it in the kind of crystalline accent that used to be employed by lady TV announcers. 'I'm glad you told me, Bob, how *good* Guinness tastes!' ... 'Hmm, you're right, George, Guinness *does* taste good!' ... 'Why didn't you tell me about Guinness before, it tastes *wonderful!*'

There was also a rather more working-class Miss with a polished Cockney accent who told her Tom that 'he'd never said a truer word' when he told her that Guinness tasted good.

Press advertising in the late fifties reflected this trend with women describing Guinness as 'marvellous!' and 'heavenly!'.

'Thank you, Mike,' said a young lady in one advertisement 'for teaching me how *good* Guinness tastes'. On the wall behind Mike's girlfriend could be seen the latest poster from Gilroy. Initially, Guinness had been doubtful about the design, because they felt that a crocodile was far too sinister a character to be used. Eventually, however, the reptile's genial expression, twinkling eye and crocodile tear were sanctioned, and one of the best of the animal posters made its appearance in the summer of 1957.

The following year, Gilroy produced a new Strength poster, featuring a tuba-player, that went through an interesting series of developments before reaching its final form.

Increasingly, however, artists other than Gilroy were designing posters. The most celebrated of these was a brilliantly simple design based on the letter 'G' by Abram Games (the artist who had devised the Festival of Britain logo). From its first appearance in 1957, it won award after award in Helsinki, Lisbon, New York, Stockholm and Barcelona, all of which is the more staggering when one realises that Mr Games sketched his original idea on the back of a bus ticket! (See page 134.)

In 1959 Stanley Penn designed a second Election poster – 'Guinness as usual during alterations' – and caused a minor furore when some people expressed the opinion that the phrase 'during alterations' actually implied

'Thank you, Mike, for teaching me how <u>good</u> Guinness tastes!'

Above: **Advertisement for women's magazines (1957), featuring one of Gilroy's crocodile posters** (*see also left*). *Below left:* **General Election poster (1959).**

Above: **Two early studies by John Gilroy for his 1958 'Guinness for Strength' poster (*right*). This poster is said to have been a favourite of Lord Alexander of Tunis.**

uinness

that Guinness was forecasting that the Macmillan Conservative Government would not be returned to office.

Alterations were also taking place at Guinness. A few years earlier, for example, the first non-Gilroy animal posters had begun to appear, with Tom Eckersley's sea lion topiary and Ray Tooby's picture of toucans in their nest (with a reminder that this was the beginning of the TV era).

The Guinness birds and animals took part in a Guinness Popularity Poll, a series of press advertisements, in which cartoon creatures interviewed real people about why they drank Guinness (a vague attempt to unite the diverse aspects of Guinness advertising). An ostrich with a microphone asks a man in a bar 'When did you drink your first Guinness?', the man replies: 'About the same time that I smoked my first pipe.' And a young woman, asked by a toucan with a reporter's notebook, to describe the taste of Guinness, says that 'It's a more-you-drink-it, more-you-like-it taste.'

About this time a penguin began a short-lived career with the menagerie, promoting Draught Guinness which was introduced regionally in 1954, and only advertised nationally a decade later when it was generally available. The penguin was devised by Stanley Penn, who told Gwyn Norris, then production assistant in the Guinness advertising department, that it was intended to immortalise them both: Penn – Gwyn. The penguin evolved, in fact, from the fount which was designed for Draught Guinness by Misha Black of the Design Research Unit. This equipment was intended to accommodate the trade-department's desire for a tap placed as high as possible in order that the barman could see what he was doing, but when the all-white fount was shown to the Guinness Board, Lord Elveden pointed out a basic flaw in the design. 'It looks like a urinal,' he observed, 'It's even got a flush at the top.' A blue panel was quickly inserted to counteract this unfortunate appearance. Blue was chosen because, at the time, it was by chance the traditional Guinness colour (being the colour of the gates at the Dublin Brewery). In addition to reflecting the shape of the fount, it was also hoped that the penguin would suggest that Draught Guinness was a 'cool' drink, particularly suited to hot weather.

Despite a number of promotional gimmicks, like little plastic penguins that waddled along table-top or bar, the character was dropped in 1965, by which time the other animals were also on the way out.

The penguin was a newcomer, but it was the oldest member of the menagerie, the toucan, who helped advertise the other major innovation of the fifties – canned Guinness.

In 1958, the Guinness animals – or rather real animals of the Guinness species – went on

Toucans in their nests agree
GUINNESS is good for you
Open some today and see
What one or Toucan do

show in the Wellington Pier Gardens at Great Yarmouth. Under the supervision of popular zoologist George Cansdale, Guinness decided to exhibit sea lions, kangaroos, pelicans, toucans, tortoises, alligators, a kinkajou and a pair of bear cubs. Each animal had a sign in its cage showing the poster that had made it famous. The project was not without its odd disasters. For example, during a raging storm on the first night, two Californian sea lions escaped, and outflanking Mr Cansdale (who tried to stop them with a deck-chair) dived off the end of the pier. Despite such initial setbacks, the zoo managed to survive and remain popular until the 1960s.

The year 1959 was important, marking as it did the Brewery's 200th anniversary. A new label was designed, and this was featured on a special Gilroy poster.

Guinness had much to celebrate; not only had the lease on the Dublin Brewery still 8800

Opposite: **The famous – somewhat over-praised – 'G' poster by Abram Games (1957). Artists other than Gilroy began designing Guinness animal posters, including (*above*) Ray Tooby (1957), and (*overleaf*) Tom Eckersley (1956).**

Lovely day for a
GUINNESS

ECKERSLEY

How grand to be a Hornbill

In 1955, Gilroy was commissioned to design some Guinness posters that could be used in Borneo where they would be hand-painted on to hoardings. Gilroy produced a number of sketches depicting native animals and birds: the wild pig, the lucky magpie and the hornbill whose horny beak was believed to have aphrodisiac qualities – a reputation which, in Africa, it shares with Guinness. The local belief that there was 'a baby in every bottle' prompted Gilroy to cast the hornbill in the role of Mr Stork – an idea which was, coincidentally, thought of to mark the birth of Prince William of Wales over twenty years later.

Although, in the event, the Borneo campaign was not used, some of Gilroy's curious sketches are reproduced here, for the first time.

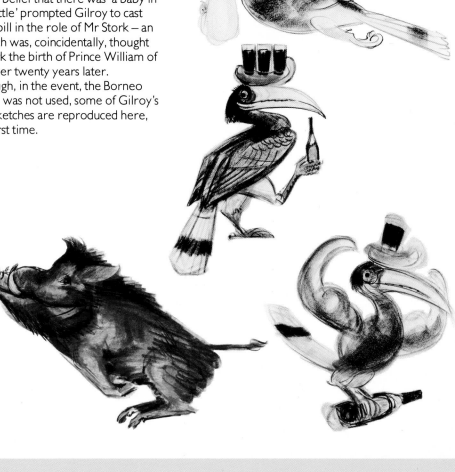

They'll be pleased
to draw you a
REAMY DRAUGHT
GUINNESS

IT'S OPENING TIME

FOR

Canned
Guinness

Right: **First Irish Guinness poster (1959).**

years to run, but within the thirty years of advertising the Guinness sales figures had gone up and up. While Dublin continued to supply Guinness to Scotland, Wales and the north of England, Park Royal was supplying Guinness to the southern half of Britain. Guinness export figures showed remarkable success, with overseas trade developing to a point where Guinness Breweries would soon be open in various parts of the world.

Guinness celebrated its bi-centenary with a day's festivities in Dublin (including Children's Races, Fancy Dress, Irish Dancing, a

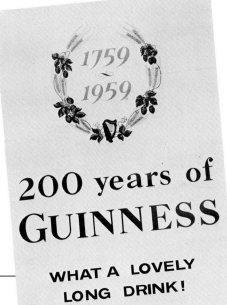

1759
~
1959

200 years of
GUINNESS

WHAT A LOVELY
LONG DRINK!

137

1759 ～ GUINNESS ～ 1959

Bicentenary Day

Programme of Celebrations at St. James's Gate Brewery
and Iveagh Sports Ground, Dublin

11th JULY 1959

GUINNESS TIME

Bisontenary Edition
1959

Baby Show and a Cut-and-Style Competition for Frocks). The cover of the programme was designed by Gilroy, as was that for the 'Bisontenary Edition' of *Guinness Time*.

At Park Royal there was a garden party and sports day, followed by a firework display that created pyrotechnic pictures of toucans, sea lions and ostriches.

The bi-centenary year saw an important development with the decision to advertise Guinness in its native land. An earlier attempt had been made in 1951 with 'Guinness is good for you' advertisements on the side of Dublin's buses. Hugh Beaver, then managing director of Guinness, explained that the advertisements were intended not for the locals but for the tourists, 'If you went to Mecca,' he said, 'you'd expect to see some quotations from the Koran' – but on buses? The Dubliners themselves were baffled, one told *Time* magazine: 'Next somebody will be telling us we should eat spuds.'

There had been one or two press advertisements that were mainly concerned with either inviting tourists to visit Dublin's famous Brewery, or telling them little-known amazing facts about Guinness production: 'First take 60 000 tons of malt,' began one, while another showed a man ordering '1 000 000 000 pints of Guinness, please'. This figure represented a year's output ('clear indication of the popularity which has made Guinness the largest

brewers in the world'). However, despite this enormous sales figure, Guinness were very much aware of an increasing public demand for ales and lighter beers.

Anticipating competition, Guinness decided to try and protect their share of the market with an organised advertising campaign. The celebrations of 1959 gave them a good excuse to begin advertising without undue notice being taken of them.

S. H. Bensons sent Stanley Penn on an atmosphere-absorbing tour of the Irish Republic. He was accompanied by the newly-appointed advertising manager for Ireland, Ken Tyrrel. They were, Penn later recalled, 'somewhere in the Ring of Kerry on the way to Killarney, when I thought of the slogan "200 years of Guinness – what a lovely long drink".' As with the first UK advertisement, back in 1929, it was just a beginning.

On the hoardings of Britain, during 1959, a new 'Guinness for Strength' poster appeared. Drawn by Harry Stevens it was visually bold but thematically tasteless.

It was, as it happens, prophetic. The whale was the last animal to be added to the Guinness zoo, and the first to be literally killed-off – on every hoarding in Britain. Within two years, the rest would suffer a similar fate – though not in public. Guinness advertising had undergone many changes but none so revolutionary as that which it now faced.

Above left: **Programme for the 1959 Bicentenary celebrations in Ireland, designed by Gilroy.**
Above right: **Gilroy's 'Bisontenary' cover for** *Guinness Time* **saw the belated introduction of a new Guinness animal.**

Opposite: **Gilroy had sketched an idea for a diver carrying a whale early in the 'Guinness for Strength' campaign, but it didn't become a poster until 1959, when it was drawn by Harry Stevens.**

GUINNESS
for Strength

Guinness in Eccentric Circles

Guinness continued producing Christmas books for the medical profession throughout the fifties and sixties, which included two striking examples of British humour at its most eccentric and whimsical, from those masters of the absurd . . . Rowland Emett and Gerard Hoffnung.

Emett, whose Far Tottering and Oyster Creek Railway cartoons had taken on reality at the Festival of Britain, was commissioned, in 1958, to illustrate *Hobby Horses*, a book of verses by Stanley Penn about curious pastimes. Emett recalls visiting the Park Royal Brewery and being struck by the fact that large numbers of sparrows ('at least 55 000 of them!') were flying around the interior of the huge cathedral-like brew-house. 'Whether or not they had anything to do with making the Guinness, I cannot quite remember.'

Emett later designed a wondrous Time-Weather-Machine as a sequel to the Guinness clock, with clouds that rained into upside-down umbrellas. But although Guinness liked the idea, they unfortunately doubted Emett's ability to build it, and sadly *Hobby Horses* remains his only contribution to Guinness humour.

Gerard Hoffnung — cartoonist, raconteur, tuba-player — had achieved wide popularity with his Hoffnung Music Festivals and his little books of musical cartoons. Like Emett, Hoffnung's odd, gentle humour was very English. In 1959 he was commissioned to illustrate *Reigning Cats and Dogs: A Guinness Book of Pets*, with verses again by Penn. However, Hoffnung died that September (at the untimely age of 34), before he was able to complete the work. Art director, Bruce Hobbs, lovingly laid out the book in such a way that it did not appear obviously incomplete. The illustrations which Hoffnung finished demonstrate so clearly how well he and Guinness went together, that one regrets the brevity of their association.

Opposite: **Cousin Hugh, the fromologist who collected cheese labels (because cheese went so well with Guinness!), drawn by Emett (1958).**
This page: **Two drawings by Hoffnung (1960): the torpid tortoise who got 'revved-up' on a cup of Guinness, and Dr Johnson with his cat, Hodge, who 'always had oysters for tea'.**

MAN!
YOU'VE EARNED THAT
GUINNESS

GUINNESS
-HIM
STRONG !

13

BREAD
OR CIRCUSES

It is quite astonishing, but despite spending almost £1 million a year on advertising, no one at either Guinness or S. H. Benson really knew who actually drank Guinness. They had opinions about the matter, of course: some people thought that Guinness was a predominantly female drink (the life-blood of elderly charladies and their ilk), others thought that everybody drank Guinness. But nobody knew for sure, because since Oswald Greene and Bobby Bevan first went on their investigative pub crawl in 1928, nobody had bothered to try and find out.

Arguably, there was no reason to do so since Guinness advertising appeared to be doing its job efficiently and effectively. Guinness production in 1936 had been 750 000 barrels; by 1956, that figure had rocketed to 2 000 000 barrels.

During the fifties, other brewers were moving more and more forcefully into the market, and were using national advertising to a far greater extent. 'Roll out Red Barrel' and 'Double Diamond Works Wonders' were among the new beer slogans, as was 'There's a promise in a glass of Mackeson', with which Whitbread advertised their rival to Guinness.

At Guinness, euphoria about rising sales-figures was muted by anxiety as to whether or not this market position had anything to do with advertising. But how could they find out? British companies were increasingly following American example and turning to consumer research to identify existing and potential markets. In 1951, despite opposition from those who thought the exercise was a waste of time, Sir Hugh Beaver, the managing director of Guinness, commissioned national surveys on Guinness consumption from Gallup and Mass Observation. The results were, to many, surprising. Guinness, it seemed, was predominantly drunk by men and those men were older than had been expected.

It took some time for Guinness to decide how to respond to these findings. There were those at Bensons who felt that effort should be put into attracting younger drinkers to Guinness, while there were those at Guinness who believed that their product was a drink to which people 'graduated' with age – rather, as someone remarked, like deaf-aids and rupture appliances! In an effort to try and find out which of these views was correct, Guinness called in George Wigglesworth, who had worked with the British Export Trade Research Organisation for five years, and who now set about the business of serious, detailed research into Guinness drinking. While this was happening, things went on much as before, with stylish designs, old slogans revamped and the obligatory touch of humour.

On television '5 million a day' provided the motivation for a series of commercials that stressed a hard working, masculine image for the Guinness drinker. Films showed shipwrights, crane drivers, trawlermen and steel workers:

'Tapping an open-hearth furnace at one of the largest steel works in Britain is Second-Hand Spud Murphy. Working with steel is *real* work and when shift's over Spud'll be ready for a *real* drink – a Guinness! Clean, strong flavour, rich, creamy head. 'Ave a Guinness and you'll know you've 'ad summit worth drinking! No wonder 5 million Guinnesses are enjoyed every day.'

Although clumsy and self-conscious, these commercials were paving the way for a whole new approach to advertising arising out of Wigglesworth's research. At Bensons, Bobby Bevan who was still chairman tended to apply yesterday's approaches to present-day situations (to the extent, for instance, of adding his smiling sponge Guinness-face as a postscript to commercials like that about Spud Murphy). However, a group of gifted young men with revolutionary ideas, were rising within the Company – they were Hugh de Quetteville, Mike Constantinidi and the late James Cameron. At Guinness, Tommy Marks was promoted to managing director of Harp Lager Ltd in 1961, and was succeeded as advertising manager by Alan Wood, who had previously managed the advertising for Hovis. While Tommy Marks had been more concerned with

Opposite above: **The first photographic poster to feature an actual Guinness drinker (1963) and** (*below*) **a poster by 'Wilk' (1961), representing the more traditional approach which it replaced.**
This page: **Poster by Abram Games (1960).**

administration – believing that to have interfered with Bensons would have been like having a dog and barking oneself – Alan Wood was to be closely involved with the future development of Guinness advertising, and instrumental in pushing not only for more research but for the application of that research to marketing. The creative personnel at Bensons responded to Wood's initiative with enthusiasm and eventually carried Bobby Bevan with them. In 1961, two posters appeared that marked the transition from one style of campaigning to another. The jovial tone of both belied the painfulness involved in that transition.

With John Gilroy's last poster, the Guinness animals ran away to sea and never came back. With Tom Eckersley's bold 'after work' device, there began a campaign directly inspired by George Wigglesworth's research studies.

Wigglesworth had enlisted the aid of Doctor F. E. Emery, an Australian psychiatrist at the Tavistock Institute of Human Behaviour, an author of a paper on 'Differences between the Communication function of the Mass Media'. As one commentator has put it, 'from then on not a motive was to be left unturned'.

Doctor Emery divided drinkers into three categories: 'social', 'indulgent' and (borrowing a term from Freud's disciple Melanie Klein) 'reparative'. It was among the reparative drinkers, Doctor Emery maintained, that most Guinness drinkers were to be found. Emery's findings were taken on board by Guinness, and Alan Wood told Bensons that some 'painful discards' would have to be faced. He was talking about the animals. He was quickly supported by de Quetteville, Constantinidi and art director Bruce Hobbs, who had all expressed the opinion that it was time for the animals to go. Budgets did not allow for a multiplicity of approaches. Guinness advertising, it was said at the time, could continue to produce circuses, or it could produce bread – it could not produce both. Guinness decided in favour of bread. The circus left town.

'The reparative,' says George Wigglesworth, 'emerged as a conscientious, controlled drinker, a good citizen and a good family man, a man who bore the burden of life ungrudgingly and whose reward was a quiet drink alone, or with his mates, at the end of the day. It was a magnificent copy platform.' A copy platform that produced the 'after work' theme – a natural development of that early intuitive 'good for you' campaign which was coming under increasing attack from those who believed the slogan to be untrue.

The reparative theme was launched in 1961 with the very first photographic Guinness poster (see p. 146).

The two would-be Guinness drinkers are conspicuously working and middle-class,

reflecting a concern to appeal to all classes – though it is interesting to note that in the first draft for the design the businessman was standing on the workman's shoulders! A poster the following year, drawn by Bruce Hobbs, was similarly self-conscious in its attempt not to be self-conscious about class!

On television, the reparative theme began with a diverse group of workers from farm, factory and office, singing 'After work we all agree, Guinness is what we need'.

This series quickly matured into one which used words rather more precisely and economically, and which was voiced by a narrator with a slow, sophisticated – almost seductive – voice: 'The Floodlights. A great crowd. The end of a great game, and now for a drink. Step inside and have a Guinness. Steady. The-re's a Guinness for you. Clean tasting. A touch of bitterness. That's Guinness. Good for an

Guinness at a crossroads. Two posters from 1961: (*above*) the last to be designed by John Gilroy, and (*opposite*) the 'new look' by Tom Eckersley.

after work
GUINNESS

ECKERSLEY

evening out and so good for you.'

Farmers left their tractors and workers their factories and made for the nearest pubs: 'A day's work done. Time to get inside and have a Guinness. Steady. Lo-vely. There's a Guinness for you. A splendid drink ...'

There was, however, a good deal of nervousness about the use of the phrase 'a touch of bitterness'. Alan Wood maintained that public taste was moving away from sweet products, and cited the phenomenal success achieved by Schweppes with its introduction, in 1957, of Bitter Lemon. In the event Wood was proved right, but several members of the Guinness Board took a lot of persuading.

The photography in these commercials was of a quite exceptional standard, and the lingering way in which the crown cap was taken off, and the Guinness was seen smoking slightly before being poured slowly into a glass, had a satisfyingly salivatory effect. Particularly when accompanied by a haunting, slightly melancholy, end-of-the-day tune, and a commentary comprised of Guinness pearls of wisdom from the past: 'Why not try a Guinness a day', 'You will enjoy proving Guinness is good

Left: **Which social class should be on top? A problematic poster from 1961.**
Opposite: **One of a series of posters designed by Bruce Hobbs (*insert below*). This shows a working-class drinker, others depicted a city-gent and a housewife.**

Putting a Bold Face on it

ABCDEFGHIJKLM
NOPQRSTUVWXYZ
1234567890?!.,

Speaking of the Hobbs-face, Benson's former art director, Bruce Hobbs says, 'I wanted to have something that had a feeling of authority about it, but that at the same time had an elegance and was capable of being used in every conceivable way in which it might be required.'

As it was first designed, the type face had a rougher texture that suggested, perhaps, stencilled lettering on hop-sacks. This style was used for some while, before being smoothed out a little, a process which Hobbs rightly feels lost some of the original character of the type face. Nevertheless, his original concept of elegant authority remained, containing as it does a hint of inspiration from the street signs of Paris.

The colours, of course, were generically Guinness – black and cream being a reflection of the drink's body and head, and red being derived from that legendary ruby gleam that lingers within the glass.

EVENING
GUINNESS

LATE EXTRA

...corded instance ...being con... ...tinent of ...inherent ...ened in ...when a ...fficer of ...who was ...he Battle ...ed in his ...had con... ...anything ...strength.

...icularly bad ...London, a ...the bus and ...ness. The bus ...when he came ...blic house. Back ...for another five ...iting—and the man ...ff again for—a

Guinness. Yes, the bus was still waiting — but he decided to walk.

THE excavation of old mining and pioneer towns in the Western States of America has brought to light a number of hand-made stone bottles clearly marked with the name 'Guinness Stout'. It seems certain from this that Guinness was well known in the U.S.A. as early as the 1850's.

THE German 'Iron Chancellor', Bismarck, is said to have been partial to *Black Velvet*, a fifty-fifty compound of Guinness and Champagne. This drink, a wonderful pick-me-up, is still extremely popular. Sometimes the rather less exotic tonic water, or cham-

pagne cider or perry is mixed with Guinness.

Reports of the value of Guinness as a hair tonic and a furniture polish have been received, but Guinness is still in most common use as a beverage on its own.

A PIECE of scrub in the thick bush, some twelve miles from Lagos, the federal capital of Nigeria has been cleared for the construction of a Guinness brewery. This new plant is designed to produce over fifty million bottles of Guinness a year. With the exception of a number of technically skilled members of the home staff, the brewery will be manned entirely by Nigerians.

EH

for you', 'Guinness – there's nothing like a Guinness', and so on. These advertising films, with their Guinness drinkers quietly enjoying their reward for a hard day's work were an astonishing development, when one remembers that only a few years earlier a Guinness advertisement had been something that featured a Keystone Cops chase with a sea lion.

From these commercials grew a series which used soft-focused camera work to transform dockyards, oil refineries and aircraft plants into blissfully idyllic settings. As the sun went down, these centres of hyper-activity were seen as being quiet and peaceful. 'This,' murmured the narrator, 'is the best bit of the day – when it's nearly over. I look at it and lock it all away before I go off for a Guinness. And Guinness is part of it. The best moment of it. Now – at the quiet end of the day – Guinness...'

Although these evocative commercials were among the most visually striking of their time (and were certainly the most direct advertising of Guinness for some years), there was a feeling that they were drifting dangerously towards exclusivity. As one former Guinness executive has put it: 'The advertising suggested that you had to be very seriously committed to Guinness in order to be able to drink it.' Edward Guinness, then sales manager in the North of England, went even further. He said Guinness advertising had become 'like the British Museum: everyone liked it and regarded it as part of the nation's heritage, but never used it.' Market research suggested that some drinkers did, indeed, find the Guinness image too remote and clubby. The real problem now was in deciding how to interpret and act upon each new set of research findings, without becoming slavishly reliant upon them. In any event, it was decided that a change of mood was urgently called for.

The lonely romanticism of locked up shipyards at sunset was abandoned in favour of intimate shots of Guinness bottles slowly emptying into glasses. There was also a change in the narrative emphasis from *my* Guinness to *your* Guinness: 'Guinness – That Guinness – Your Guinness – Strong, dark, deep, rewarding – That Guinness – *Your* Guinness – There's nothing else like it.' Guinness advertising was changing beyond all recognition.

In 1962, the new men with their new vision for Guinness won their final victory, when they succeeded in transforming the Guinness poster. In the early sixties, the poster hoarding was still a major form of advertising, but increasingly featuring photography rather than artwork. Alan Wood presented the Guinness Board with a choice of directions. One was represented by a new poster design by Gilroy showing a man about to enjoy a Guinness after working in the garden, the other comprised a series of posters, designed and

photographed by Bruce Hobbs, showing bottles, glasses and the words 'Good for you'. There was no doubt as to which approach was favoured by Wood, de Quetteville, Constantinidi and Hobbs (though Bobby Bevan doubtless felt a distressing pang or two), the doubts were centred on how the Guinness Board would react. In the end they chose the photographs and set a final seal, as it were, on the future of Guinness advertising.

Photographing a Guinness wasn't that easy and Hobbs recalls trying to last out a photosession by faking a Guinnessy-looking head with egg-whites. Nevertheless, photography was here to stay and the old days of 'commercial art' were at an end – for the time being at least.

In 1963, Bobby Bevan retired. It was at once both a disaster and a golden opportunity. A disaster in that Bevan's personal philosophy and charisma was completely bound up with Benson's public image. A golden opportunity because the old regime was finally at an end and the new men could be given free rein.

Two decisions were taken that were to be of immense importance to the future development of Guinness advertising. Firstly it was decided that the Guinness image needed

Above: **Scenes from the TV commercial 'After Work' (1961).**

Below: **Photographic poster by Hobbs (1963).**

revitalising and consolidating. In the thirties, Guinness had had clearly recognisable style in its use of colours, lettering and layout. But during the war and post-war years that all-pervasive style had disappeared, and any number of colours and type faces were now being used. It was a fact that the Guinness name seldom looked the same in any two advertisements, posters or commercials.

A renaissance now took place, with Bruce Hobbs master-minding a revised corporate image, centred around a new style of lettering that is still, today, known by its designer's name – 'Hobbs-face'. The Hobbs-face was introduced on a poster depicting the first ever serious portrait of a Guinness drinker. The photograph was an early commission from the now celebrated photographer Terence Donovan. 'Man!' it said in sixties parlance, 'you've earned that Guinness' (see page 142).

There was about this slogan a feeling as of a sigh of relief, and doubtless there were those involved in the advertising, who really did give a sigh of relief when it finally reached the hoardings, for its progress there had not been without incident. There had been a great deal of debate about what the Guinness drinker should be like. How old was he? What class did he belong to? Ironically, it was the same problem that Guinness had faced in the 1930s when the idea of a Guinness family had been conceived and then abandoned in favour of the animals.

The early proofs of the poster were closely scrutinised. Wasn't he rather too young? Wasn't his hair rather too long? Wasn't his raincoat rather too creased? And were his fingernails rather too clean? In the end, however, the Guinness drinker appeared, although few people realised just how revolutionary was his presence on the poster hoardings of Britain. No doubt there were odd murmurings in a few Gentlemen's Clubs to the effect that Guinness seemed to have adopted a rather curious way of advertising lately, and a few people may have wondered where the funny animals had gone, but even if Guinness had been aware of such sentiments, they would undoubtedly have remained resolute. They had come to terms with the fact that they were entering a whole new era of advertising and marketing. The 'Man' poster was proof positive of that.

Thirst-stop Guinness

From 1956 onwards, Guinness produced a number of advertisements to be used on the sides of buses. Some of these long, thin posters were adaptations of current advertising; others – like Bruce Hobbs's joke about standing the bus on end – were devised especially for their mobile sites.

14.

THERE'S A CHANGING WORLD IN A GUINNESS

Advertising wizard David Ogilvy once remarked that 'Buying is a serious business. Nobody buys from clowns'. Guinness had made the decision that their days of clowning were at an end, and certainly no one could accuse them of failing to take their business seriously.

Research into who drank Guinness (and why) was carried out by Public Attitudes Surveys, an organisation headed by George Wigglesworth.

'What might have seemed to the public somewhat pedestrian advertising, after the great days of Gilroy,' Wigglesworth has written, 'was saved by a technical and aesthetic excellence.' It wasn't, perhaps, so much that Guinness advertising was pedestrian as just a little *too* serious. Compensation was offered with a series of mosaic posters featuring the occasional smiling drinkers.

These were a development of a series of extraordinarily confusing 'stream of consciousness' posters that comprised an unreadable maze of Guinnessy words printed in

Hobbs-face. On hoardings these gave the appearance of having been pasted-up by someone who was drunk. The idea worked rather more successfully in a series of special press advertisements, each of which had a selection of words that had a mix of associations with Guinness and with the publication in which they appeared. For example, *The Listener* carried an advertisement featuring such words as High Frequency, Balance, News and Sound; while the *New Statesman* had a jigsaw design made up of Honourable, Ovation, Vote, Measure and Constitution.

In Ireland the same idea was used and a special poster of Joycean words was designed. Guinness drinkers had also appeared on Irish posters in 1963, with a silk-screen design that, in its bold use of flat colour, was exceptionally striking. On some sites, however, rain caused the colours to run, and the managing director of Guinness axed the poster as an unsatisfactory exercise. There was additionally some anxiety about the wording – 'Guinness – that's a drink and a half!' – since in Ireland 'a half' usually refers to a measure of whiskey which many drinkers would order as a 'chaser' to a pint of Guinness.

For the most part, in order to ensure the best standards of reproduction, posters lithographed for the UK market were imported and occasionally overprinted with new slogans.

The Horse and Cart was one of a very few Gilroy posters to be used. It was actually his most internationally successful design, being as easily understood in Malaya as it was in the Republic of Ireland.

Guinness's continued overseas development

Opposite: **Guinness poster for lateral thinkers (1965)** (*left*) **and press advertisement for** *The Economist* **(1965).**
Right: **Irish poster (1962).**

151

– the Ikeja Brewery was opened in Nigeria in 1963 and the Sungey Way Brewery in Malaysia in 1966 – brought about the formation of Guinness Overseas Limited. Most Guinness advertising overseas consisted of cinema and television commercials, using the reparative themes. Some of these films were quite bizarre, the most astonishing of all being a cartoon commercial, featuring a little man shipwrecked on a desert island with a beautiful girl. He has no interest in life until a bottle of Guinness floats by, empties itself into his mouth and restores him Popeye-style to full virile life, whereupon he uproots the one tree on the island and builds a hut from it. He disappears inside, dragging the girl with him and stays there for days on end. When a ship finally arrives to rescue him, he refuses but asks, instead, for a crate of Guinness. As the film ends he retreats to his hut once more, with his Guinness – and his girl!

There were comparatively few Guinness posters overseas, most advertisements being hand-painted by signwriters – a process which on one occasion resulted in the startling copy-line 'Guinness ... that's *god*.' This, surely,

must be the most ambitious advertising pitch of all time!

In the overseas press, Guinness advertisements were still predominantly using artwork – and in particular, an affectionate line in caricature.

It is curious, but these jovial advertisements appeared in the same year as the sober Guinness men began appearing on posters in the United Kingdom.

In 1966, a simple – but highly significant – poster went on display throughout Britain. It represented a major breakthrough in the development of the Guinness product.

It was the first ever national campaign for Draught Guinness made possible by the development of the 'easi-serve' cask which incorporated a chamber for the gas needed in dispensing the beer. One reason for the poster's significance was that it began the standard practice of using Draught rather than bottled Guinness to represent the product in advertisements. There were those at Park Royal who wondered if it was altogether wise to associate Guinness almost exclusively with the public house drinker. They need scarcely

Why is a daily GUINNESS good for you?

1 Guinness gives you *satisfaction!*

2 Guinness gives you *power!*

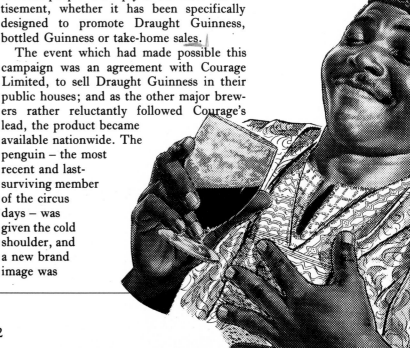

3 Guinness gives you *happiness!*

A Daily GUINNESS is good for you

LN-GU 31-8860

have worried, since a Guinness advertisement to most people is simply a Guinness advertisement, whether it has been specifically designed to promote Draught Guinness, bottled Guinness or take-home sales.

The event which had made possible this campaign was an agreement with Courage Limited, to sell Draught Guinness in their public houses; and as the other major brewers rather reluctantly followed Courage's lead, the product became available nationwide. The penguin – the most recent and last-surviving member of the circus days – was given the cold shoulder, and a new brand image was

Opposite: **Nigerian advertisement (1967).**
Above: **South African press (1966).**
Above right: **UK poster (1966).**

Overleaf: **Poster celebrating the 900th anniversary of the Battle of Hastings (1966).**

strong dark rewarding

GUINNESS

sought and developed by Alan Wood and the staff at Bensons. The new black, buff and red colour-scheme was adopted, and the hand-blown, distinctively shaped Waterford tankard became the symbol for Draught Guinness.

Guinness representatives were educated about the new campaign. 'There is,' they were told, 'an intimate and inseparable relationship between the tankard and the product ... A special bright and friendly colour-scheme has been created and this has been adhered to throughout the range *... These fundamental points obey the principles of good, modern advertising.'*

There were, however, a few minor hitches, not least of which was the question of what the new tankard should be called. 'Tankard' was thought likely to cause confusion with the Whitbread draught beer of that name, so other possibilities were considered. An Irish expert suggested Curran, Cruiskeen Law, and Cuppawn; while Bensons suggested a string of such fanciful alternatives as Bumper, Stouter, Sorter, Gatesman, Bombard, Guerdon, Sicer, Garnet, Grenado, Stoup, Hanap, Mazer, Skimmer, Grenadier Mug and Dubliner. Although there would have been an undoubted charm about ordering a garnet of Guinness, none of these suggestions were either suitable or feasible. In the end it was decided that the receptacle was a 'Waterford glass tankard', though everyone – logically – just called it the tankard!

The Draught revolution was a serious business (sales rose from 30 000 to a million barrels within a decade) so it is not too surprising that

Guinness adopted a serious tone of voice at this time. Perhaps a little too serious, since one thing that almost everyone involved in changing the Guinness image is now agreed upon is that the lack of humour was regrettable. There was little or nothing to leven the grimly conscientious selling that to many seemed so strange after countless years of puns and quips and gags.

In 1966, there were two brief glimmers of light-heartedness. Firstly a poster with a label-less bottle obscuring part of the Guinness name. This look-twice brain-teaser, devised by Bruce Hobbs, was both an imaginative and effective advertisement – it also invited the observer to smile (see p. 156).

The same year saw Stanley Penn's last poster idea, devised to celebrate the 900th anniversary of the Battle of Hastings. The poster with its minutely adjusted version of the Bayeux Tapestry was phenomenally successful. Every new poster brings letters from the public asking for copies, but this one brought over 8000 such requests and the smaller versions of the poster were reprinted several times. The full-size bills are now expensive collectors' items (overleaf).

Many people were quick to observe and comment upon the curious fact that one of the chargers appears to have a human foot. This, Guinness claimed, was not a mistake on their part but an actual feature of the original tapestry. That, however, is not the case. They were, perhaps, misled by one of the many inferior copies of the tapestry in print, but if any doubt remains, it can be dispelled by reference to Eric MacLagan's 1943 book *The Bayeux Tapestry* (Plates VII and XLIV). The glass of Guinness in the hand of the knight riding the odd-footed horse was, of course, nobody's mistake! The popularity of the poster continues with a reproduction of the design now available on a bath towel – particularly suitable, no doubt, if you were to go bathing at Hastings!

The success of the Bayeux poster prompted a design for Irish advertising, depicting Ireland's great folklore hero, Fionn Mac-Cumhaill and his hounds fighting the cyclops.

In the press there were several attempts to raise a smile or two, but compared with the good old days it was a largely solemn, cerebral sense of humour.

The Guinness acrostic was part of a long-running series of brilliant, yet coldly contrived, verses written by *Punch* humorist, Paul Jennings. An accomplished verse-writer, Jennings lacked the genial good humour of John Trench and the homely warmth of Stanley Penn. By this time, Trench had moved on to work on other accounts, and with Gilroy gone, Penn remained the last bastion of the old Guinness stronghold.

Stanley Penn, like Gilroy, had served

Guinness well; without his clever ideas and witty turn of phrase, Guinness advertising would have been less memorable. His great misfortune was to be overtaken by a changing world and a changing profession.

As the sixties drew to a close, change was very much in the air. For ten years Guinness had been thoroughly researched without any statistical evidence actually being found to support the once-hallowed 'reparative' hypothesis. It had, nevertheless, achieved its aim – recruitment of drinkers to Guinness had improved, and sales-figures were continuing to rise. But by 1968, there were people both at Guinness and at Bensons who felt that the theme was too restrictive, and that Guinness should appeal to a wider audience. There resulted a campaign based on the slogan 'There's a whole world in a Guinness'.

'There was,' writes George Wigglesworth, 'a sort of *Guinness Book of Records* feel about it.' Which is as good a description as any. The posters were much the same as they had been for the past ten years – bottles, glasses and close-ups of Guinness drinkers, only the captions had been changed. On television, however, full use was made of the new theme. Each commercial comprised a subtly-edited montage of library film footage, every scene of which was accompanied by a one-word caption that sometimes reinforced the visuals and sometimes created an interesting tension with them.

'There's a whole world in a glass of Guinness ... Enthusiastic (cheering football crowd), Smooth (skiers), Surprising (skiers falling over), Friendly (heavyweight wrestler thumping his opponent), Clean-tasting (high divers), Strong (karate champion) and Reassuring (sunlit trees).'

The music used for these commercials was ironically entitled 'Take, oh take those lips away'. The campaign proved directionless and ineffectual. 'It was,' George Wigglesworth has said, 'back to the circus but without Bevan's genius as ringmaster and without Gilroy as performer.'

Bevan and Gilroy had gone, so by now had Penn. Trench was doing other things, and Bruce Hobbs had left Bensons to work for David Ogilvy in America.

The post-Bevan era at Bensons was a difficult one, with struggles to restructure the Company's finances and an embarrassing degree of in-house fighting. Bensons had lost its presiding showman. Guinness account directors, Hugh de Quetteville and later Mike Constantinidi did much to bring Bevan's approaches and philosophies into the modern age. But Guinness became uneasy, anxious no doubt because of apparent uncertainties at top-management level where a succession of managing directors had come and gone in a relatively short period of time.

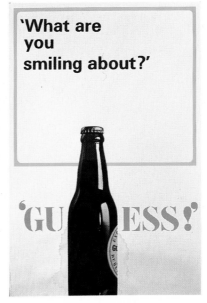

Top: **Posters from 1966 and 1968.**
Centre: **Scenes from TV commercial 'The World of Guinness'.**
Left: **Ireland's equivalent of the Battle of Hastings poster, featuring the legend of Fionn MacCumhaill (1966).**

Bensons has been described at this period as being like a post-revolutionary state where coups happened daily. These power-struggles were highly damaging to Benson's reputation, and several major accounts had already moved to other agencies when, in 1969, Guinness finally decided that it was time for a change.

Micky Barnes, who had the ill-fortune to be the then managing director of Bensons, writes in his autobiography *Ad: An inside view of advertising* – 'At the time of the parting, Bensons were offering a service and creating advertising that was as good as, or better than, any it had produced for Guinness in the forty years it acted for them.' But Guinness had lost confidence in Bensons, and Bensons, as a result, lost Guinness.

Gilts are up: but will the £,
Unchanged against the $,
In Zurich now regain lost ground?
No economic scholar
Needs to tell us yet again
Exports must do better:
Stout should be our effort, then...
Stout our whistle-wetter.

Jenningsness

Paul Jennings's association with Guinness began as a result of the three-monthly lunches which the Guinness Board used to give for people in the literary and artistic world. Among the guests at these lunches were such people as Barnett Freedman, Charles Mozley, Hugh Casson, Patrick Campbell and Jennings. It was at one of these lunches that Jennings had suggested the idea of the Guinness Poetry Award which was given annually for some years.

His advertising contributions were specially commissioned in order to provide one-off advertisements for magazines dealing, as Jennings says, with 'anything from cricket to stock broking'. His astonishing prolific output during this period fell into three basic categories. Firstly, the acrostic poem – 'I discovered the eight letters of "Guinness" ideal for this' – a device which Jennings perfectly mastered (despite the singular difficulty imposed by the letters in the name). Secondly, he produced a number of quatrains using the words 'Good for you'; and thirdly, a staggering number of advertisements which catalogued the qualities – all of which ended with 'ness' – required by various groups of people. Fishermen required resourcefulness, calmness, quickness, readiness and naturally, *Guinness*.

Q. *What do cricketers require?*

A. *Cricketers require suppleness, eyesight, boldness, flannels, quickness, sunshine, Englishness, pavilions, keenness, tea, fairness, spectators, left-handedness, turf, W.G. Gracefulness, sight-screens, right-handedness, bails, deceptiveness, unflinchingness, sloggers, centuries, mellowness, pubs, gregariousness, Ashes, goodness, and* **GUINNESS**

G.E.4432

Mozart is good for the masses
Schönberg is good for the few
Souza is best for the brasses
But **GUINNESS** is good for **YOU**

Give him a Guinness!

15

BUT I DON'T LIKE GUINNESS!

The advertising industry was astonished. It seemed practically inconceivable. Guinness and Bensons had been together for forty years. Most people had supposed them to be inseparable. From the beginning, Bensons had devised for Guinness some of the most distinctive advertising ever created; and, at the end, had made valiant attempts to meet its client's frequently changing requirements. Nevertheless, confidence between agency and client had been irreparably damaged by Benson's in-house problems, and there was doubtless the feeling that, only when Guinness were free from Bensons, would they really be free from what was now considered the out-moded heritage of the past.

As a result, Guinness began seeking an alternative advertising agency. Almost 40 companies were approached for discussions before a shortlist was drawn up, and the choice finally narrowed down to two agencies – London Press Exchange and J. Walter Thompson. LPE made a strong bid for the account, but the Guinness Board favoured JWT. J. Walter Thompson was an American-owned agency, with a large and very profitable London branch and a reputation for highly stylish advertising. Although part of a huge enterprise, J. Walter Thompson's British directors and staff were able to offer Guinness the stability and creativity that they had once received from Bensons.

Guinness invited Thompsons to prepare a new advertising campaign for presentation to the Guinness Board within three months.

Bensons were invited to make a new presentation at the same time, but they were doubtless rather unnerved by the fact that during those three months, members of the Guinness staff worked closely with Thompsons, giving them research data and information to help their preparations. To all intents and purposes it was as if Bensons had lost the account before they had even made a bid to save it.

Thompsons made their presentation to the Guinness Board and, two days later, were asked to handle the account. 'It was only then,' says managing director Jeremy Bullmore, 'that we really believed we had the job.' The copywriting team was headed by Bullmore and featured two rising talents in the industry, Tom Rayfield and Chris Wilkins. The success of Thompson's presentation was undoubtedly due to their pilot television commercials which were imaginative and uniquely 'Guinness'. In the decade and a half since ITV had begun broadcasting, the main emphasis of advertising had shifted from posters to televised commercials. It was the one area where Bensons had felt least confidence, and where Thompsons particularly excelled. Within ten years, their Guinness commercials became as celebrated and popular as had Benson's classic posters.

The first commercial to appear was entitled 'Champagne' and was photographed by top

Posters from 1971 (*opposite*) **and 1970** (*below*).

159

fashion-photographer Terence Donovan. It showed a bottle of Guinness covered in cobwebs in a cavernous wine cellar: 'When champagne is first put into a champagne bottle, it is not quite champagne. Only when it's had time to ferment and mature naturally inside the bottle does it become champagne. One of the very few other drinks they make that way nowadays is – this one ...'

Thompsons achieved two vital objectives with their first series of commercials. They placed Guinness squarely in the beer market, reinforced its uniqueness, and began challenging some of the prejudices that existed about Guinness. Where Guinness advertising on television had previously always been thematic – 'End of the Day', 'World in a glass of Guinness' – JWT opted for a series of individualistic films that highlighted various aspects of Guinness. The 'Champagne' commercial concentrated on the specialness of the drink, as did a film which suggested that Irish coffee had been inspired by the appearance of a glass of Guinness. The idea that Guinness was drunk by the mature and the discerning provided the inspiration for a simple, yet extremely forceful commercial that gave teeth to Guinness television advertising for the first time.

A series of drinks was seen on the screen, each accompanied by a distinctive sound: baby's feeding bottle – baby gurgling; bottle of school milk – school children singing; bottle of 'pop' – jukebox; glass of beer – rugby song; Guinness – convivial pub sounds. Then came the punch line: 'It's good to grow up!'.

In a sense, J. Walter Thompson were using material that had been around and had been used since Guinness advertising first began. It was the approach to that material which was significantly new.

They returned, for example, to the subject of Arthur Guinness's famous 9000 year lease on the Dublin Brewery. The flamboyant Guinness signature was seen being made with a quill pen as the following commentary was heard: 'When Arthur Guinness first brewed Guinness in 1759, the world was not quite ready for it. And, for many years, Arthur Guinness had to brew ordinary beers as well to make ends meet. But, as the centuries passed by, the world grew up and people began to understand the strong, dry taste of Guinness, and now over six million glasses of Guinness are served every day. But that's just the beginning; you see, when Mr. Guinness first brewed Guinness, he signed a lease for the brewery – and the lease was for 9000 years.'

Thompson's television commercials had a striking simplicity after the fussiness of Benson's last efforts. They also used the short time available to establish the unhurried quality of Guinness, with measured commentaries complementing shots of slowly filling glasses:

'Every Guinness you drink comes in two parts – the black part and the white part. The whole point about Guinness is that you drink the black part *through* the white part. That's the only way to get from the roasted barley, malt and hops the proper smooth, dry taste that comes only from Guinness. That's why it takes both the black part and the white part to make a Guinness.'

'With our initial advertising,' says Jeremy Bullmore, 'we were trying to say "Come closer to Guinness", trying to find how close we could actually get, using television, to the experience of drinking Guinness without the physical meeting of the beer and the lip. Making people salivate at the aesthetic experience of watching a Guinness being drawn.' All of which Thompsons did with great style.

If these commercials had a fault, it was that they offered no models with whom the potential Guinness drinker could identify. People, it was decided, had to be got into the advertisements again. In 1970, a now legendary commercial appeared. It was the first to feature the Thompson breed of Guinness drinker. It was also the first to be shot in colour.

A coach is seen taking a high-spirited group of people on their company's annual outing. They are singing 'Blaydon Races', and enjoying all kinds of drinks from oddly-shaped bottles. 'The annual outing,' says the narrator, 'is much the same every year – but, whatever the others drink, the real lads stick to beer. And the beer they prefer is the most popular beer in Britain. The trouble was, last year, they ran out. So, this year – they're taking a little extra.' The camera pulls back to show a pipe leading from the back window of the coach to a Guinness tanker which is following behind.

The Guinness drinker and his drink was soon being shown within the context of the public house, and Thompsons excellently captured the lively atmosphere of the pub, with its humour, camaraderie and competitiveness, its culture and its odd characters.

A man is seen slowly drinking Guinness. Another man dashes up to him, panic-stricken.

'I just heard that the Martians have landed at Stoke Newington and they're ravaging the whole countryside with their death rays.'

The drinker continues to enjoy his Guinness, unperturbed, while his companion goes on with his story.

'Macclesfield has been razed to the ground and the Greater London area has had to be evacuated. And the Isle of Man's sunk – sunk without a trace!'

'Last orders, Gents, please,' calls the landlord.

'Oh,' says the drinker, sadly, 'that's a pity.'

In another commercial, two young foreigners attempt to order a Guinness, but

Tall, dark and have some.

GUINNESS

Poster (1972) featuring one of J. Walter Thompson's more outrageous puns.

Press advertisement presenting Guinness as a black wine (1972).
Overleaf: Press advertisement designed for magazines and colour supplements (1974).

Red, white or black?

GUINNESS

have difficulty saying the name. They ask for 'Gwynse', 'Gwinnse' and 'Gwense' before seeing someone get a Guinness by asking for 'The usual'. They then order 'Two usuals'!

In 1971, Guinness used their engaging pub folk to help introduce drinkers (and bar staff) to the idea of having a cool Guinness. Looking at the beer market, Thompsons were struck by the fact that Guinness was increasingly the only brand not found on the cold shelf. They tentatively suggested that it should be. Guinness themselves – who had spent forty years trying to educate the publicans of Britain that Guinness should be served at room temperature – were, not surprisingly, horrified by such blasphemy. The idea, however, was an

How to play Guinness

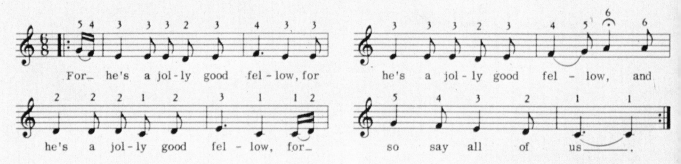

It is a well-known fact that everyone who drinks Guinness is fond of music. (This is one of the reasons we put a harp on every bottle.) So here is a simple, do-it-yourself instrument that is fun to make, and even more fun to take apart.

All you need is a bottle-opener, two drumsticks, and a dozen bottles of Guinness.

Open all the bottles. Take the first, summon all your will-power and set it aside untouched. Take the second, have a small sip and put it next to the first. Have a slightly larger sip from the third bottle, and carry on until the amounts in the twelve bottles range from full to empty in equal steps.

If you're not careful, you will do this properly first time. With a little effort, however, you can do it wrong and have to start all over again.

Finally, though, you'll have to admit that you've got everything sorted out, and you can then begin to play your "Guinnessphone".

Take up your drumsticks and tap the bottles experimentally. You will discover, much to your amazement, that the twelve bottles make up a full musical scale. (Should you tip one over, simply replace it with another bottle containing the same amount of Guinness. Little mishaps like this are bound to happen now and again and are known in the trade as "accidentals".)

You should now be able to dash off a couple of quick choruses of "Drink To Me Only" and "For He's A Jolly Good Fellow", by the end of which opening time will probably be fast approaching.

Finally, you can drink your instrument, adjourn to the pub and tell your friends about your new hobby.

DRINK TO ME ONLY

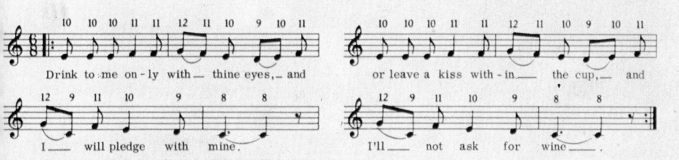

Coming shortly: instructions for making an organ out of old bottle-tops and powered entirely by Draught Guinness.

SPECIAL OFFER!

Dark Beer from Arthur Guinness Son & Co. (Park Royal) Ltd.

This unique and interesting beverage, designed for us by our founder, is now offered to readers as this week's special selection. This remarkable beer, which has remained virtually unchanged since 1759, is brewed naturally and is fashioned from the finest ingredients: hops, yeast, barley and pure water.

and is easily portable. It is also easily drinkable and available in a variety of sizes.

It is a beer for the dining room, sitting room, conservatory or garden, and is suitable for television viewing or entertaining.

We are happy to be able to offer this excitingly different drink to readers at a price very little higher than they would expect to pay for it elsewhere. (In fact, the only other places one could buy it are the 78,000 or so pubs throughout the country, not forgetting clubs,

off-licences, supermarkets, hotels and restaurants.)

How to order

Complete the coupon (in block capitals) and enclose your (signed) cheque made out to 'Cash'. Do not bother to fill in the amount; we shall be happy to do this for you. If you are not pleased with your purchase we shall flatly refuse to believe it.

Please do not return any purchases to us; we have plenty. Allow up to 2 years for delivery.

Finished in attractive black with contrasting white top, it fits well into any surroundings

---

Guinness special selection 'Dark Beer' ORDER FORM.
I enclose cheque left obligingly open and made out to cash.
I am over 18.
Please send me, subject to availability...............barrels of Guinness (minimum order 100 barrels)
Please tick colour choice here
☐ Black ☐ Black ☐ Black
Please also tick preferred second choice

Name...
....
Address.......................................
....
....
....
Town..
County...

If you wear glasses please put tick here ☐

Reg (and Arthur) in England.

PLEASE CUT

important one, since 'cold' meant 'contemporary', and Guinness needed to be thought of as a contemporary drink. An experimental campaign, therefore, was run in a chosen area of the country and the results were monitored. Those results were so favourable that cold Guinness was advertised nationally and became extremely popular.

The commercial that instigated cold Guinness featured a rather wet and ineffectual character who pops into a pub to speak to the landlord. 'Excuse me,' he begins, rather nervously, 'I'll be looking in tonight and I'd like an ice-cold Guinness, please.' 'A *what*?' asks the man behind the bar. 'An ice-cold Guinness – you know, cold like ice – I like it.' 'Well,' says the landlord, 'you're not drinking it here. Cold Guinness! Stone me!' 'This is my brother,' replies the young man, and a huge character, who might well be a heavy-weight boxer, enters the bar. 'He likes cold Guinness, too.' The landlord does a double-take and swallows hard. 'Two cold Guinnesses? Certainly, sir. They'll be ready for you this evening, sir.'

As they leave the bar, the brother gives the landlord a parting smile, 'See you, then!'

There was no doubting the fact that Thompsons had achieved enormous success with Guinness advertising on television. Less successful, however, were their first posters. They had sought hard to find a contemporary

poster artist who could produce the modern-day equivalent of Gilroy's classic posters. Only when no one suitable could be found did they resort to photography. The earliest slogan, running from 1969 to 1971, was 'Give him a Guinness', a light-hearted variation of the concept of Guinness as reward. The difficulty was that the ideas and the photographic treatment of them were too subtle to be quickly grasped and appreciated on poster-sites. This was a pity since there were some amusing ideas in the series: a shoe-shop assistant surrounded by dozens of ladies' shoes; a fireman at the top of his ladder with a tiny kitten on a branch, and a do-it-yourselfer who has hung a picture but who has four fingers of one hand bandaged up! One poster showed a home-decorator hanging wallpaper with a detailed galleon design, one strip of which was upside down. A quick glance at the poster was insufficient to understand its story, and, to make matters worse, the wallpaper made it difficult to read the slogan. Nevertheless, the poster had some admirers, and several people wrote, asking for parts of the poster with which to wallpaper their living-room! (See p. 159.)

Within two years, Thompsons had found their feet and established the fact that they had an inspired knack for devising brilliantly witty slogans that placed Guinness in a setting – 'The Inn Drink' – or suggested its suitability

At this time of year, there are a great many visitors in our country from abroad. Since these foreigners are probably unfamiliar with our great British institutions, such as Wigan Pier, Windsor Castle, Leeds United and Guinness, we offer this small guide to one of these institutions.

If you are yourself a foreigner and unable to read English, please stop reading this now and ask a bobby or metermaid to explain.

THE FIRST STEP.

On arriving in England and looking around, your first reaction will be "Mon mot, J'ai soif" ("My word, I need a drink"). Whether you've landed at London Airport or by rowing-boat on the Romney Marshes, this should not be a problem.

There are 78,000 places to get a drink in Britain which we call 'public houses'. As far as we know, every single one of them is equipped to serve you Guinness. You will find them

divided into rooms called "Public Bar", "Snug", "Parlour", "Smoke Room", "Lounge Bar", "Saloon Bar", "Tap Room" and sometimes just "Bar". Chacun a son bar. Every room will serve you beer.

Go in. Approach the counter and say "Guinness please". Or, if you prefer draught beer, "A pint of Guinness, please!" And you've taken the first step to understanding England.

Give me a Guinness

'Mon Dieu'

IF IN DOUBT ABOUT YOUR COMMAND OF ENGLISH, CUT THIS OUT AND SIMPLY HAND IT TO THE BARMAN.

THE FIRST TASTE.

Guinness is unlike the beer you are used to drinking, just as Englishmen are unlike you. Take the first sip slowly; it might help to close your eyes. Concentrate on the strong, dry taste. And don't give up.

By the time you've drunk half your first Guinness you'll begin to understand. Order a second one, and you'll begin to be convinced. By the third Guinness, you may even like it.

In fact, Englishmen like it more than any other beer. But they, of course, have had the advantage of living here all their lives.

CLOSING TIME.

England is not perfect. After we lost a battle in the First World War, our Government decided that public houses must close in the afternoon, and again well before midnight, to protect the population from themselves and keep the Industrial Revolution revolving.

This law has never been repealed. So you, too, will be protected while you are here.

Outside licensing hours, you can drink in the privacy of your caravan or tent or whatever by obtaining Guinness from an 'off-licence'. These shops will sell you as much Guinness as you can carry away. As long as you're over 18 years old.

A Foreigner's Guide to Guinness

FOR DRAUGHT DRINKERS ONLY.

Guinness comes not only in bottle, but also as a draught beer. In fact Draught Guinness drinkers sometimes play a traditional English game on foreigners like yourself. This is how it works.

An Englishman comes up to someone foreign-looking and says: "I'll bet you the price of a pint I can write my initials on the top of a pint of Draught Guinness, drink it all, and still have my initials left at the end."

So you take the bet, he takes out a broad-nibbed pen and it all works out just like he said. Be warned: this 'head-test' is not a trick, but something we've been doing in the brewery for years.

Try it. Then look for an unsuspecting Englishman! "Cheers" as we say in our country.

THIS IS THE SHAPE THE WORLD WAS INVENTED GUINNESS...

Your own country may not have been invented. But then, Guinness has changed a lot of things in the last 211 years. In fact, Guinness is now

IN BEFORE ARTHUR GUINNESS

sold in 130 foreign countries. So if Guinness becomes a habit while you're here, you won't have to break it when you get home.

A GREAT YEAR FOR GUINNESS.

In your own country, you probably pay a great deal of attention to vintage years. So, in ours you will wonder which Guinness vintage to ask for.

You will know, or have been told, that the last exceptional year for Burgundy was 1959, for Claret 1961, for Port 1963 and for Champagne 1964.

The last exceptional year for Guinness was undoubtedly 1970, but then so was '59, '61, '63, and '64.

In fact, the only Guinness vintage to avoid buying is 1758. This was a very bad year indeed, because Arthur Guinness did not invent Guinness until 1759.

So spend lots of your funny foreign money on Guinness and we'll all have another good year.

One of a series of advertisements for Guinness appearing in the colour supplements this year.

FOOTNOTE: Now, perhaps the only other thing you need to understand is the British sense of humour.

as a summer drink – 'Just the weather for dark glasses'. Using this format, Thompsons reintroduced the idea of Guinness as an accompaniment to food – 'Red, white or black?' – and offered its first serious challenge to the non-Guinness drinker with the searching question: 'Are you afraid of the dark?'

Sometimes, their puns were too smart for their own good. 'Summer pints (and some are bottled)' was the first of an occasional series of jokes that went over most drinkers' heads. However, simplified visual designs and clever copy resulted in some much-loved and long-remembered advertisements.

With an increased proportion of the advertising budget being spent on television advertising, there was a gradual reduction not only in poster designs and sites, but also in some press advertising. Notwithstanding which, Thompsons saw that press and magazines

Press advertisement by Erté (1974).

offered special opportunities to them, both in underlining the message of their television and poster campaigns and in resuscitating the quirky humorousness of Guinness.

Much of Guinness's press advertising at this time comprised extensive text, in direct contrast to the ever-shrinking poster slogans.

Thompsons gave Guinness advertising a quality it had never really possessed with Bensons – sophistication. In 1974, the great Russian-born French designer, Erté (Romain de Tirtoff) was commissioned to produce designs for the eight letters in the name, Guinness. The mythical characters which he produced appeared on double-page spreads in the classier periodicals, accompanied by the simple caption: 'It's always been good to look at.'

Once Thompsons had discovered how well this sophisticated image suited Guinness, they

There are some drinks that men 'expect' girls to drink.

When he asks you what you're going to have, you can almost hear him filling in the answer for himself.

And nine times out of ten you'll give him the satisfaction of guessing absolutely right. Unless you ask for something 'unexpected'.

Many of you drink Guinness at home, knowing Guinness is full of good, natural ingredients.

However, lots of you have found other reasons as well for asking for something 'unexpected'. It seems that the dark, inviting looks and strong, natural taste of Guinness are just what you wanted.

Advertisements for women's magazines: (*opposite*) 1976; (*right*) photographed by Barry Lategan, 1974 (detail); (*far right*) 'WHO SAID "Men seldom make passes at girls with glasses"?' also photographed by Lategan, 1974 (detail); (*below*) photographed by Harry Pecinotti, 1973.

decided to direct it towards a specific audience with a stylish campaign for women.

Guinness advertising to women has always been a barometer for social attitudes. In 1939, the copy was unashamedly domesticated: 'The tragedy of the evening meal is that, so often, the woman who's cooked it finds she doesn't want to eat it.' A few years later it was aimed at those women who were having to do a man's job and, in the post-war years, it began to reflect the increasing independence of Britain's womanhood. During the sixties, women were largely forgotten – they didn't fit

too comfortably with the tough, rugged, masculine image that Guinness had acquired. It was in the 1970s, when much was being written about the liberated, professional woman, that Guinness found a new way of talking to the ladies:

'It takes a bold girl to ask for a Guinness in a bar full of men. Try it next time you're in your local. Watch the raised eyebrows. And ignore them. After all, if men had had their way, girls would never have been allowed in pubs at all. So demand your rights.

'Women have been enjoying the dry and distinctive taste of Guinness for two centuries now, and it's time to stand up and be counted.

'And who knows? If enough girls start drinking Guinness in pubs, it might even become respectable. Then you'll have to think of something even more daring to do.'

The Guinness women's campaign was largely the brainchild of Thompson staff-member, Ann Leworthy, who, in her choice of clothes, make-up and hair styles for the models, not only reflected contemporary fashions but frequently anticipated them. These advertisements were photographed by some of Britain's finest photographers, including Barry Lategan and Harry Pecinotti.

The series had a strong initial impact – Guinness all but became a fashion accessory for the trendy seventies girl – but there was no lasting conversion of women to Guinness, and the cost of achieving this short-term success was probably too high. Nevertheless, the

campaign was a popular one – particularly with men, who enjoyed looking at beautiful girls, beautifully photographed and who were pleased to see Guinness in such attractive surroundings. There may not be any statistics to prove it, but these advertisements probably had more impact on men than all the old men-in-raincoats posters put together. There was certainly something very reparative about many of them!

The view of women reflected in these advertisements was also to be found in a television commercial of the period, entitled (without any chauvinistic motivation) 'Final Say'. The scene: a pub. The characters: Mike and his girlfriend, Liz. They are playing darts. Mike throws his; it hits the board and falls on the floor. He walks towards the camera, shaking his head.

MIKE: I don't believe it!

CAMERA: What'll it be then, Mike?

MIKE: Oh, I'll have another Guinness.

CAMERA: And, er ... what about, er ...

MIKE: Liz – want another?

LIZ (who has just successfully thrown a dart): Oh! Fine, won't be a sec.

MIKE: That's two, then.

CAMERA: What? Guinness?

MIKE: Mmm ...

CAMERA: You mean you both drink it? Come on!

MIKE: Sure. We have for quite a while now.

CAMERA: Bit of gentle persuasion, eh?

LIZ: Well, it didn't happen overnight!

CAMERA: I'll bet! How did you manage it then?

LIZ: Well, I finally got him to try one!

Guinness advertising has seldom been more courageous than in the early to mid-seventies, and there is no better example of that courage than a campaign launched in 1973 to seriously challenge non-Guinness drinkers by appearing to criticise the product.

The television commercial showed a young man in a pub who buys his friend a bottle of Guinness and (keeping his hand over the label) asks him what it is.

FIRST MAN: There you are. What's that in there, then?

SECOND MAN: I don't know. You've got your hand over the label.

FIRST MAN: Well, smell it!

SECOND MAN: Beer. It smells of beer.

FIRST MAN: Shut yer eyes.

SECOND MAN: *What??*

FIRST MAN: *Shut yer eyes!*

(He does so.)

SECOND MAN: What yer doin'?

FIRST MAN: Pourin' it out fer yer.

SECOND MAN: Come on. Stop messing about, will yer?

FIRST MAN: There y'are. You drink that!

(He does so.)

FIRST MAN: Well?

SECOND MAN: Yes, it's all right, that. Not a bad drop of beer, that.

(He opens his eyes and his friend reveals the label on the bottle.)

SECOND MAN: GUINNESS?! But I don't *like* Guinness ...

In the thirty years since the war, the world had changed dramatically – so, clearly, had Guinness advertising. Whoever would have thought that Guinness would have used such a slogan, or that the sacrosanct drink that, for so many years, had been lovingly described in language that tested the ingenuity of the most literate copywriters would ever have been described as 'not a bad drop of beer'?

Outrageous! And devilishly ingenious!

A daring poster caption introduced to accompany a television commercial on the same theme (1973).

"I've never tried it because I don't like it."

A date with Guinness

Every Christmas the licensed trade eagerly awaits the arrival of the new Guinness calendar. The first of these, illustrated by Tony Escott, appeared in 1970 and, since then, many leading illustrators and cartoonists have contributed to these attractive point-of-sale advertisements.

"It's from Guinness Mr. Caxton. They want a calendar."

GUINNESS JANUARY 1973	SUN	MON	TUE	WED	THU	FRI	SAT
		1	2	3	4	5	6
	7	8	9	10	11	12	13
	14	15	16	17	18	19	20
	21	22	23	24	25	26	27
	28	29	30	31			

The Bear and Ragged Staff

GUINNESS MAY 1974	SUN	MON	TUE	WED	THU	FRI	SAT
				1	2	3	4
	5	6	7	8	9	10	11
	12	13	14	15	16	17	18
	19	20	21	22	23	24	25
	26	27	28	29	30	31	

Vive Le Guinness

APRIL 1975	SUN	MON	TUE	WED	THU	FRI	SAT
			1	2	3	4	5
	6	7	8	9	10	11	12
	13	14	15	16	17	18	19
	20	21	22	23	24	25	26
	27	28	29	30			

GUINNESS

SEPTEMBER						
SUN	MON	TUE	WED	THU	FRI	SAT
					1	2
3	4	5	6	7	8	9
10	11	12	13	14	15	16
17	18	19	20	21	22	23
24	25	26	27	28	29	30

Clockwise: **Mike Williams, 1973; Thelwell, 1974; Giles, 1978; Don Roberts, 1975.**

Instant Guinness

AMAZING SCIENTIFIC BREAKTHROUGH!

And they said it couldn't be done! For years, scientists all over the world have laboured in vain to solve mankind's oldest and most baffling problem: how to print Guinness onto newspaper. But now a solution has been found. Dr. Patrick O'Brien of our own research division has, after several days of more or less continuous thought, perfected a foolproof system. You can be the first to sample his handiwork, and it won't cost you a thing.

In the bottom right-hand corner of this advertisement you will see a panel marked 'Drink this Space'. All you have to do is cut it out, follow closely the instructions which Dr. O'Brien has provided, and enjoy a long, satisfying drink of the world's very first instant Guinness.

The secret of the process lies in those tiny dots which cover the panel (you can see them quite clearly with a magnifying glass). Each dot contains, for the technically minded, approximately 0.0000073645 grammes of the highly concentrated Guinness molecule Trididublinbruriate which combines with a glassful of ordinary water to produce Guinness of unparalleled quality. So find yourself a pair of scissors and a glass and away you go. Cheers!

Here's how to make your instant Guinness:
1 Using a pair of sharp scissors, cut out the panel in the right-hand corner of the page. Find a clean glass as tall as the panel (it's important not to use any container which is not made of glass, since this could interfere with the delicate balance of the molecules).
2 Roll the panel into a cylinder **with the tiny dots on the outside** and stand it on end inside the glass. It should unroll slightly and cling to the glass, leaving a space in the centre.
3 Gently fill the glass with water, pouring it carefully into the centre of the cylinder. Use tap water if you prefer Draught Guinness, but pour the water from an empty milk bottle if you like bottled Guinness.
4 Leave for three minutes until the head forms and carefully withdraw paper from Guinness.

If at the end of three minutes, the water has not turned into Guinness, discard it entirely and proceed to your nearest pub, off-licence or licensed supermarket where you can purchase a fairly instant Guinness of the more usual variety.

① ② ③ ④

DRINK THIS SPACE

IMPORTANT

Complete this form before making your instant Guinness.

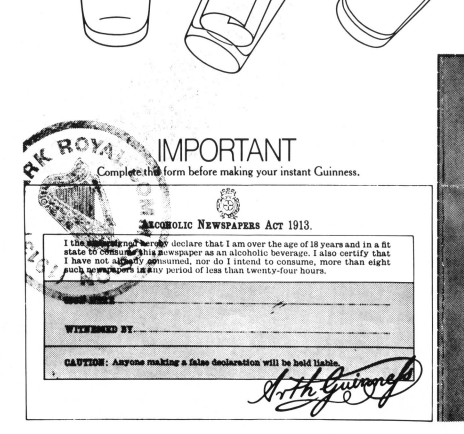

ALCOHOLIC NEWSPAPERS ACT 1913.

I the undersigned hereby declare that I am over the age of 18 years and in a fit state to consume this newspaper as an alcoholic beverage. I also certify that I have not already consumed, nor do I intend to consume, more than eight such newspapers in any period of less than twenty-four hours.

WITNESSED BY

CAUTION: Anyone making a false declaration will be held liable.

16

A LITTLE DARK REFRESHMENT

In 1971, a press advertisement revealed a staggering breakthrough in Guinness technology that looked set to transform the entire brewing industry – instant Guinness! It comprised millions of tiny printed dots of concentrated Guinness. All you had to do was cut out a square of instant Guinness, place it in a glass and add water. Anyone trying this experiment would have found that, as the water saturated the paper, the words 'April Fool!' became visible. The advertisement had appeared on 1 April, and quite a few people were actually taken in by it – including a number of inmates in Pentonville Prison, who, reputedly, collected dozens of copies of the advertisement in the hopes of having a secret binge!

In 1977, Thompsons produced another brilliant gag for inclusion in *The Guardian*'s special April First supplement on the floating islands of San Serriffe. The advertisement showed an unlikely glass of Guinness with a white body and a black head, and the following explanation:

'It was after the freak barley crop of '56 that the local inhabitants of San Serriffe first began to notice a change in their beer.

Opposite: **Press advertisement, 1 April 1971.** *Below:* **Poster by Hugh Harkness (1975).**

The taste was the same. It still poured slowly and evenly. But the white head turned out black, and the strong dark body was white.

Experts put it down to the novice farm helpers who spent their holidays in San Serriffe that year.

Knowing little about crops, they sowed the barley seeds upside down.

Not until the brewing process was nearly completed did the Head Brewer discover the mistake. By which time it was too late.

Faced with disappointing thousands of loyal Guinness drinkers he took the now historic decision to continue to brew.

For twenty years San Serriffe kept their secret. Indulging themselves in a Guinness that was truly unique.

Now, to coincide with their emergence, San Serriffe has decided to export a special celebration bottle. Their loss is the world's gain.

Guinness, as brewed in San Serriffe, should shortly become available in your pub, club and bar.

You'll know it by the special label on the bottle, and of course it's instantly recognisable when you pour it out.

However, if you'd like to be one of the first to try a San Serriffe Guinness we'll happily send you a free conversion kit.

To get yours, cut out the coupon, putting it upside down in the envelope for easy sorting, and send it to San Serriffe Guinness Export Dept., 6 or 9 Turnover Strasse, Park Royal Brewery, London NW10 7RR.'

Anyone who kept that edition of *The Guardian* now has a much sought-after collector's item. In 1981, the same paper was pulling people's legs again – this time with a report that a United Kingdom Weather Authority had been created to control the British climate. Guinness took the opportunity to announce their intention of opening a tropical nature reserve on Romney Marsh, called Toucan Park, and to advertise for the post of its Head Keeper.

Dozens of applications were received, and every applicant was sent an apologetic letter explaining that the scheme had had to be abandoned for the next several thousand years, and an exclusive T-shirt with the legend: 'I was fool enough to apply for the job of Head Keeper at Toucan Park.'

Thompson's topical Guinness advertising was superb – in 1970, they produced their first election poster – 'Guinness for P.M. (or even earlier)' – and a clever accompanying press advertisement, with a caption that advised 'If you are over 18 there are two things you can do today.'

In 1972, they produced an ingenious parody of a Government announcement about the

TODAY'S MENU
Ploughman's Lunch
Shepherd's Pie
Steak & Kidney Pudding
Ham Salad
Scotch Eggs
Cornish Pasty
GUINNESS GUINNESS

introduction of petrol rationing; and, in 1973, they marked the bi-centenary of the American Declaration of Independence with an amusing speculation on how Arthur Guinness might have viewed the matter two hundred years earlier.

The bi-centenary advertisement was one of a series of simple, yet stylish illustrations by Geoff Dunbar that used the blackness and whiteness of Guinness to create a distinctive form of advertising that was suited to the pages of the daily press. Although these advertisements were easily read and understood, Guinness received considerable criticism from people who felt that they lacked the polish of their television commercials. Among the special subjects featured in this series of adver-

tisements were Valentine's Day – 'Don't forget the one you love'; Leap Year – 'If she offers to buy you a Guinness today, accept her proposal'; and Friday the thirteenth – 'For good luck let something black cross your path today.'

This series also included the first advertisement for Guinness shandy: 'Guinness Shandy. It's unthinkable but not undrinkable. Cooled draught Guinness and lemonade mixes really well. And tastes even better than that. In summer, in the glass, the lemonade makes the black part lighter, and the white part even creamier. And once you've tried a cool Guinness shandy you may ask if there are any other ways of mixing Guinness.' This advertisement had a coupon with which to send for a copy of

Press advertisements:
Below: (left) **December 1973**;
(right) **1976**.
Opposite clockwise: **New Year's Eve, 1975**; announcing *The Guinness Blacklist*, **1976**; **marking the American Bi-centenary, July 1976**.

Something to do while the white part is separating from the black part.

Next time someone pours you out a pint of Guinness watch closely.

See the white part slowly rise from out of the black part to form that smooth, creamy head.

See the black part settle to become that strong dark body.

Guinness® is one pint you can enjoy before you taste it.

And when you taste it, you can relax.

Knowing you've all the time in the world to get one down.

If you've never had one before, try half this year

and half next.

In 1776, Arthur Guinness took the news coolly.

When he read the news in 1776, Arthur wasn't at all perturbed.

Because by that time, of course, Arthur Guinness had been independent (having invented Guinness in 1759) for well on 17 years.

A sip of cool Guinness restored his equilibrium.

And with a further sip, Arthur settled coolly down to savour the rest of the day's news.

A long cool Guinness.

There's nothing quite like it for asserting your independence.

YE OLDE **Daily Mirror** COLONIALS DECLARE INDEPENDENCE

We are not so much shaken as shattered.

The other day, we heard of a barman in St. Tropez who serves a drink which consists of a bottle of Guinness, rum and lime juice shaken vigorously and poured over crushed ice.

Now we know some people like to mix our beer with the occasional half of bitter, or even cider.

But this new development is beyond the pale. The barman in question assures us that his invention is extremely refreshing and still retains much of the distinctive Guinness flavour.

Be that as it may.

If Arthur Guinness had intended Guinness to be drunk with rum and lime juice, he'd have put them in the bottle.

So we've taken the precaution of publishing the Guinness Blacklist. It features the twenty best ways to drink Guinness, next to drinking it on its own.

You may think this is a lot of fuss about nothing, but you'd be surprised.

There's a lot of strange drinks abroad, these days.

Send coupon to: Guinness Blacklist, 107 High St, Brentford, Middx.

Please send me a free, full-colour copy of the Guinness Blacklist.

Name
Block letters, please

Address
Block letters, please

Send this coupon to:
Guinness Blacklist,
107 High St, Brentford, Middx. S3

Illustrations by Larry Franklin from *The Guinness Blacklist* **(1976).**
TUMBRIL – Guinness, port, brandy and champagne . . . in one glass! This terrifying drink is supposed to be a cure for hangovers. It is called a Tumbril because you only get into it if you feel like death!

GUINNESS SHANDY – The practice of drinking Guinness with lemonade is rumoured to have started with the New Zealand rugby team, during a British tour. After a game, they ordered *Guinness* and lemonade (mistaking it for *bitter* shandy), and found it extremely refreshing. Some say this is how they became known as the All Blacks, but it seems most unlikely.

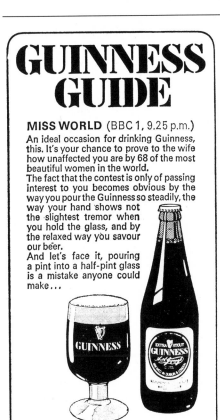

GUINNESS GUIDE

MISS WORLD (BBC 1, 9.25 p.m.)

An ideal occasion for drinking Guinness, this. It's your chance to prove to the wife how unaffected you are by 68 of the most beautiful women in the world.

The fact that the contest is only of passing interest to you becomes obvious by the way you pour the Guinness so steadily, the way your hand shows not the slightest tremor when you hold the glass, and by the relaxed way you savour our beer.

And let's face it, pouring a pint into a half-pint glass is a mistake anyone could make...

Guinness in your own good time.

GUINNESS GUIDE

POT BLACK (BBC 2, 7.50 p.m.)

We think Pot Black must be the perfect viewing to drink Guinness by.

That whispering voice and the click of ivory just oozes relaxation.

So, come ten to eight, pour one out and follow the progress of the black ball.

Each time it smooths its way towards the pocket have a reflective sip and come the end of the game when it disappears for the last time you should be on your final mouthful.

What remains on the table?

The white cue ball.

What remains in your glass?

The white head.

Funny that, isn't it?

Guinness in your own good time.

GUINNESS GUIDE

MATCH OF THE DAY
BBC 1, 10.20 p.m.
(In Scotland see Sportscene)

Just in case the ref forgets his, you bring your glasses to tonight's match.

Then while you've got them handy, carefully pour in a Guinness.

(But don't throw it in, that's a foul way to treat our beer.)

If you're viewing in black and white, Guinness is the one in long dark shorts.

You'll find that during the season most people keep it on top of the table.

So every time you hear 'cheers' from the crowd, you can raise your glass and take a sip.

And next week, you can enjoy Guinness in the Cup.

Guinness in your own good time.

Guinness television guides (1976).
Overleaf: **Posters by Gerry Preston (1976) and Mick Brownfield (1977).**

The Guinness Blacklist – a helpful guide for those willing to mix their Guinness with port, Indian tonic, orange juice, ginger, lime and various other drinks. Who on earth would want to do that, you ask? Well, over 42 000 people sent for copies, so . . .

An ingenious running series was devised for the television programme pages of the national daily newspapers. Eighty-five versions of the 'Guinness Guide' appeared between October 1975 and September 1976, featuring humorous descriptions of every kind of television programme from thrillers to situation comedies and from soap operas to sporting fixtures. The series ran consistently in the *Sun* and the *Daily Mail*, although some other papers – and the BBC – were rather less enthusiastic about them.

Among the delights of the Benson era of Guinness advertising were the thousands of advertisements produced for specialist publications. They provided an excellent public relations service for Guinness. Unfortunately, it was an expensive service. Thompsons sought to rationalise this situation by producing a series of standard photographic designs that could be given a variety of slogans to suit various occasions. All these advertisements showed tankards, glasses, bottles, cans or take-home packs of Guinness. The captions were brief and witty. 'Our opening number' (Royal Albert Hall concert programme); 'Have you graduated yet?' (University Handbook); 'Our little black number' (St Michael Fashion Show programme); 'Uniformly good' (Police magazine); and 'Now pull the other one' (first seen in the Cambridge University Boat Club programme and later adopted by the Pepsi-Cola company).

These advertisements took their inspiration from a series of posters promoting Guinness take-home sales, with such clever slogans as 'Ours after hours', 'It's nice to have a round at home', 'Opening ours?', 'You'll need glasses', 'Keep a drop by for when friends do' and 'Open at closing time'.

In 1976, advertising for take-home Guinness was given a new, slick image in airbrushed artwork. Bobby Bevan would have been delighted by the anthropomorphic beer can.

Posters for Draught and bottled Guinness mainly consisted of more puns – 'The cool of the evening,' 'A little dark refreshment,' 'It's perfectly natural' and 'Cool, calm and collect it.'

There was a tendency developing towards over-cleverness, with such slogans as 'A phew in the shade' and the inexplicable '1975 will be much the same as 1759' (which was meaningless unless you knew that 1759 was the year when Arthur Guinness bought his Dublin Brewery). The most triumphantly enigmatic advertisement to appear for Guinness during this period was undoubtedly the 1975 poster, 'Hop Squash,' which *Campaign* described as one of the worst posters ever thought up!

Two years later, Thompsons demonstrated

UNWIND

GUINNESS
AT HOME

Hop squash

GUINNESS

1952

1957

We've poured

Pint sighs

Mm...   Mmm...   Mmmm...   Aaaah.

Above: **Poster (1975).**
Opposite: **A much criticised pun from 1975, and (*below*) poster by Philip Pace, celebrating Queen Elizabeth II's Silver Jubilee (1977).**

how brilliantly the pun could be used when they produced a poster to mark the Queen's Silver Jubilee – which, like its famous predecessor in Coronation Year, cleverly omitted the Guinness name whilst leaving the observer in no doubt whatever as to who the advertiser was.

The year 1976 saw the beginning of the 'Guinness – it's as long as . . .' campaign. The first of these posters was based on a highly successful design produced for the Republic of Ireland, comparing Guinness with snooker (p. 183). It subsequently provided the scenario for a memorable television commercial that won the Grand Prix de Television at the 1976 International Advertising Film Festival.

The 'long as' theme continued with 'It's as long as the midnight movie' (showing a hairy paw about to seize a glass of Guinness), 'It's as long as a country walk,' 'It's as long as a summer evening' and (with the rejuvenated girder-man) 'It's as long as you can remember.'

The following year, the poster slogan was 'Thank goodness for Guinness' (a further variation of the old 'My goodness – Guinness is good for you' – themes) and Guinness was once more visually located in a pub setting with engraved mirrors and Guinness-coloured dartboards. Thompsons next opted for an elaborate series of advertisements, using photographs of specially hand-painted inn signs that, according to research, the public remembered without, unfortunately, remembering what they advertised.

In 1978, Guinness borrowed an Irish poster design showing a row of Guinness glasses, but changed their slogan ('Black is Beautiful') to the curiously mundane 'There's a lot of it about,' which offered little challenge to the non-Guinness drinker.

Another problem area was the campaign for women, which had recently become perilously élite: 'Smoked salmon, asparagus, a slice of lemon, a bottle of Guinness – the perfect light lunch. Natural. Elegant. Delicious. Do you really need anything else?' A new series of women's advertisements was launched featuring 'The Guinness Interview,' in which professional and artistic ladies – poets, potters and glass-blowers, jockeys and riding-instructors, zoologists and fashion-designers – were entertainingly interviewed and beguilingly photographed by Robert Montgomery. This long-running series, used both in the colour-supplements and the women's press, succeeded, by a stroke of genius, in combining the best elements of Guinness advertising to women. What could be more delightful than to know that Elkie Brooks enjoyed a Guinness in the pub while her washing was whirling around in the launderette?

'You don't have to be an incipient domestic science teacher to know that fitness means watching what you eat. At the moment Elkie is on a special diet that cuts out meat and milk: "I drink herbal teas, make my own (unfortunately runny) yoghurts, and eat lots of vegetables, brown rice and fish. I also drink

Guinness.
It's as long as a summer evening.

Guinness because I like it, and because it's a natural beer. I'm very much into natural foods at the moment. I can't stand things with additives.

"If you won't think it too boring, I'll tell you another time I like a Guinness – when I'm doing the laundry. I bung everything in the launderette, and toddle off down to the pub with a friend or a good book. Then when I've finished I go back and collect my washing. That sounds ordinary, but I really dig it."

'Even though Elkie Brooks has gone far along the road to acceptance as a rock singer, she still hasn't lost the use of a good oven:

"I could give you a marvellous recipe for Guinness. Braise some meat, pour the Guin-

Posters: (*above*) **photographed by Bruce Brown (1976);** (*below*) **by Tony Copeland (1978).**

THE MAN AT EASE

GUINNESS

ness over it, adding bouquet garni, garlic, a little brown sugar and some wine vinegar. As I'm not supposed to eat meat now, I'm trying to adapt that one. It's to go in a recipe book I'm writing, any suggestions gratefully received."'

There were a number of delightfully ingenious, and wholly original, ideas to emerge from Thompson's advertising – not least of which were their parodies of film posters, like 'A Fistful of Guinness', 'starring' Roasted Barley, Malt and Hops and made on location at Park Royal Brewery and in Dublin.

Thompsons had successfully added radio to the advertising media which could be employed by Guinness, and they produced for it some very funny and imaginative commer-

Posters: (*right*) **photographed by Tony May (1976);** (*below*) **by Tony Heathcote (1977).**

cials. One series used Frank Muir to examine great summer pastimes:

FRANK MUIR: Golf is a game where you hit a ball that's balancing on a peg an inch off the ground into a hole in the grass that you can't see, about five hundred yards away. Now, you hit the ball with a long stick which has a bit on the end of it, making sure always to hit it away from you.

Then, carrying thirteen other sticks in a kind of long carrier bag, you walk after the ball. Should you be fortunate enough to find it, you hit it away from you again.

Some people hit their ball into sandpits or streams. Others prefer the woods with its heavy undergrowth. Despite the appalling language you may hear, most people play golf to help themselves relax.

NARRATOR: Don't give yourself a bigger handicap than you have to this summer ... Try a cold Guinness ...

Other radio commercials took the form of domestic cautionary tales:

WOMAN: Well, my Lord, up until then, it was an ordinary day, really. Far as I remember, my Lord, I got up, same as usual, made the tea, woke the children, got dressed, got Fred out of bed, cooked Fred's breakfast, made his sandwiches, wrapped them up, said goodbye, swept the floor, made the beds, fed the toucan, called the plumber, ran for the bus, collected Kate, scrambled the eggs, made the toast, scoffed the lot, washed the dishes, baked a cake, collected Tom, dried the dishes, made the tea, played with the kids, fed the cat, made the supper, ran the bath, washed the dishes, bathed the kids, read 'em a story, got 'em to bed, dried the dishes and then Fred and I sat down and put our feet up in front of the telly and poured ourselves a nice couple of bottles of Guinness, lovely it was, my Lord, and Fred took a long drink of his Guinness and turned to me and said: You don't know how lucky you are, he said, not having to work, and that's when I shot him.

On television, Thompsons had continued producing witty commercials. In one of them, a young man goes down on to a crowded holiday beach with a seaside bucket full of ice and a bottle of Guinness, which he proceeds to open and enjoy. The sun blazes down and the other men on the beach, seeing the cold Guinness being drunk, retreat one by one to the nearest pub. When the pub is full of people ordering cold Guinnesses, the young man enters the pub and goes behind the bar. 'Well done, lad!' says the landlord, 'Now give us a hand here!'

That commercial appeared in 1972; the following year saw another popular and

DRAUGHT ★ set up by friends... and goes down a hero!!!
DRAUGHT ★ no holds barred!!!
DRAUGHT ★ always cool, calm and collect it!!!

Featuring tall, dark and have some

DRAUGHT!

IN

A FISTFUL OF GUINNESS

ALSO STARRING
ROASTED BARLEY, MALT AND HOPS.

PRODUCED AND DIRECTED BY
ARTHUR GUINNESS.

MADE ON LOCATION AT
**PARK ROYAL BREWERY
AND IN DUBLIN.**

GUINNESS

TASTE THE EXCITEMENT AND THE ADVENTURE AT YOUR LOCAL!

prize-winning film in which a young Welsh barmaid tries to pour her first Guinness. Two Guinness drinkers attempt to educate her, and eventually she succeeds in pouring a perfect glass of Guinness. However, the camera pulls back to reveal a large number of half-filled glasses up and down the bar. 'Whatever will I do with all these?' she asks. 'Don't worry, love ...' says one of the drinkers, '... we'll get rid of them for you!'

In another commercial, a young lady constantly quizzes her male companion about his drink. 'Why does Guinness look like that?' she asks. 'Well,' he replies, 'it's the roasted barley.' 'Why do they roast the barley?' she enquires. 'Helps the flavour,' he explains. 'Makes it dry – smooth.' 'Why smooth?' 'So it goes down easily.' 'Then why,' asks the insatiable young lady, 'is the head a different colour?' Her friend looks from his Guinness to the girl in total amazement. 'So you can tell it's the right way up.'

The situations in these commercials were always ingenious and the humour consistently infectious. For example, in one film, a man is

Opposite: **Press advertisement by Tony Coles, parodying the movie poster for** *A Fistful of Dollars* **(1974).**
This page: **Two posters by John Bantin (1979 and 1980).**

seen attempting to make home-brewed Guinness; in another, a character devises a Heath-Robinsonesque Guinness-pouring machine. In 'Food for Thought,' a barmaid offers customers in her pub a lunchtime menu of 'Shepherdspiebeanssteakandkidneytomato-cheeseandpicklesscotcheggssausages'. 'Oh, and a bottle of something to go with it,' says one young man, 'What would you recommend?' The barmaid takes a bottle of Guinness, opens it and pours a drop of it into the bottom of a Guinness glass. This she holds out to the young man and asks: 'Would sir like to taste it?'

Writing of Guinness advertising in *Campaign*, in 1979, Francis Harmar-Brown (late of Bensons) expressed the following opinion: 'Ever since television, Guinness posters have dithered all over the place. So here are some responsible thoughts to celebrate fifty years of Guinness posters. Let television do the serious, rewarding bit. Let women's magazines do the women. Let posters make Guinness light-hearted, universal, accessible. Bring back the animals. Anyone under twenty-five is just about ready for them – look at the Hobbits; look at Mickey Mouse. They'd be a cult in seconds.'

A few months later, in the summer of 1979, a very curious poster appeared on the hoardings. It showed a flock of 'penguinnesses'.

It was the beginning of an outlandish series of posters that depicted Guinness as woods on a bowling green, as chess pieces on a chequerboard, as the cars on a ferris-wheel, as parachutists dropping from the sky, and, most ludicrously of all, as the gasholder behind The Oval.

The circus was back in town.

Take up Irish history tonight

17
TAKE UP IRISH HISTORY TONIGHT

There is an old story of how an Irishman was walking down a country lane one day when he spotted a leprechaun. 'Now you've seen me in broad daylight,' said the little character, 'I must do your bidding. I will grant you three wishes. Whatever you ask for shall be yours.'

The Irishman thought long and hard, and then asked if he might have a bottle of Guinness that would never be empty. The leprechaun murmured a few strange words under his breath and waved his hands in the air. And then – pop! – a bottle of Guinness stood before the man. He took up the bottle, put it to his lips and drained it, but he had no sooner set it down upon the ground than it was once more full. Again he drank the bottle dry, and again it refilled.

'Well now,' said the leprechaun, 'what can I grant you for your other two wishes?'

'Well,' replied the Irishman, thoughtfully, looking at the bottle, 'I think perhaps I'll have another couple of those!'

Guinness is Ireland's national drink. Six out of every ten pints of beer drunk in Ireland are Guinness. And nowhere will you find more legends about Guinness than in the small, smoky, pubs of Dublin. Even there, men will tell you that Guinness tastes the way it does because it is made from Liffey water, although it is not. And anyone standing on O'Connell Bridge and looking down on the Liffey would doubtless see such things floating by as would make them glad that it is not. The water, two million gallons a day, comes, in fact, by pipeline from St James's Well in County Kildare.

Understandably, Guinness advertising in Guinnessland has to be rather special.

When, in 1969, the United Kingdom advertising account passed from S. H. Benson to J. Walter Thompson, the Irish advertising was taken over by Arks Limited of Dublin, who, for the past ten years, had advised Bensons on the suitability of their advertising for the Irish market.

Their first poster appeared in October 1969. Designed to show a glass of Guinness by an open window with the copyline 'Come on in', it eventually appeared without a slogan – and, with appropriately Irish logic, won an award for the year's best advertising copy!

Perhaps because they lived in the city of James Joyce, Arks's first major campaign consisted of word-plays on the Guinness name – beginning with the newly devised expression, 'Guinnessness'. Other 'Ness' captions followed, including: Friendliness, Summerness, and Coolness (the latter being subsequently

SOMETIMES WE FEEL THE WHOLE WORLD IS AGUINNESS

It is. So it isn't.

Homeliness

Opposite: **Cartoon by Calman (1970), Irish poster (1976).** *This page:* **Posters** (*above right*) **1971 and** (*remainder*) **1970.**

Guinnessness

Summerness

borrowed for use in the UK).

One of these slogans, 'genniuss', caused a number of people to telephone the Brewery and point out that 'genius' was not spelt the way it appeared on the poster. However, nobody seemed to be in any doubt as to who the advertiser was! Another playful variation was the classic slogan: 'Sometimes we think the whole world is a Guinness,' which is probably beyond the comprehension of anyone who isn't Irish.

Guinness had advertised on Irish television since 1961 when Radio Telefis Eireann had begun. Their first efforts were disastrously unfunny pub anecdotes which the public found 'corny' and, when repeated, 'very irritating'. These were soon replaced by the dancing animals used on British television. A sporting series began in 1963 based on the slogan, 'You've earned that Guinness,' and showing cyclists, cross-country runners and Gaelic football players.

For three years from 1966, Guinness commercials comprised fifteen to thirty second films showing scenes from Irish life, including a race meeting, an agricultural show, a fishing trawler and a St Patrick's Day Parade. 'Guinness,' said the commentary, 'is the most natural drink in the world.'

Then, in 1970, Arks began producing television commercials on the Guinnessness theme. They were sophisticated versions of the 'End of the Day' commercials previously used in Britain. In one, a coach party of trendy, young people find a welcome in a hostelry where the only drink being enjoyed is a Guinness:

'Travelled all day? Well, stop on the way.
You know what to say. Because Guinness is there.
We'd stay until darkness, but the best of friends must partness.
Don't take it to heartness. Guinness is here.
There's more than goodness in Guinness.'

Out of the 'Ness' campaign grew the idea of togetherness – of getting together with Guinness and the Guinness drinkers. A clannish image that is still a predominant theme in Irish Guinness advertising.

There was a return to humour with 'Happy Couple,' a commercial which told the story of a domineering wife who had given her henpecked husband instructions on meeting with their prospective daughter-in-law's parents. He sits gloomily in a bar with a short drink in front of him and, while his wife talks to the girl's mother and father, we hear his thoughts: '"Don't forget", she says, "we'll be with Mary's mother and father – so, for your son's sake – don't talk about horses and don't go ordering pints for everyone." Cruelty to husbands, that's what it is!'

His wife is still talking: 'Since meeting your Mary, he's been a changed lad, I'm telling you ...' At which point, the happy couple themselves arrive. 'Hello, Mr O'Brien,' says Mary, 'What's that you're drinking? Wouldn't you rather have a pint of Guinness?' 'Well,' says Mr O'Brien, avoiding his wife's withering gaze, 'I would really.' 'Well,' says Mary, 'while you're there, will you get me one, too?' A chorus sings, 'Get together with a Guinness' and Mr O'Brien adds as a postscript: 'Sure the boy doesn't know how lucky he is!'

The next commercial in the series – entitled 'Mosaic' – was the most ambitious to be produced in Ireland at that time, using a cast of hundreds. 'Get together with a Guinness' was performed by the rock group, Blue Mink, before a wildly enthusiastic audience. Interspersed with the song were shots of Guinness being poured and drunk.

Today, such an advertisement could not be produced in Ireland since new advertising codes require that no alcohol commercial should show or imply 'crowded situations and excessive heartiness and enjoyment'. Not

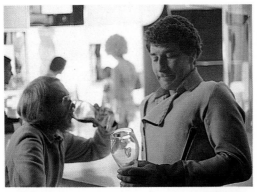

Scenes from Irish TV commercials 'Holiday' (featuring Irish spacemen) and 'Good Old Days' (1974).

more than six people may appear in an advertisement (including bar staff), all of whom must be 'clearly at least twenty-five years of age' and not more than one scene may be shown with anyone actually consuming an alcoholic drink, in addition to which, 'sound effects, background music, singing, laughter, etc., must be kept to a reasonable minimum'. Contrary to popular belief, advertisers cannot say or do whatever they please.

In 1974, Arks began a series of commercials which showed Guinness as a timeless, unchanging drink in a changing world. The drink they drank in the good old days, 'when summer really was summer and in winter the harbour would be frozen over'.

One commercial showed two Irishmen talking. 'Do you know,' asked one of them, 'my father and his father, and his father before him, they all drank it.' 'What?' asks the other. 'Guinness! And my great-grandfather lived to be a hundred – and three! There's history in Guinness.' 'Hey, I like a bit of history,' says

the other, as futuristic music is heard and we discover that the two Irishmen are, in fact, spacemen. 'Where are you going for your holidays, this year?' 'Well, the Missus wants to go to Mars, but I don't know . . .'

Some of the most effective ideas in advertising are the simplest, and one of the simplest and most effective advertisements by Arks was a commercial showing the gradual settling of a

Scenes from TV commercial 'Move over to Guinness' (1981).

pint of Guinness to the accompaniment of the slow movement from Grieg's Piano Concerto in A Minor. This blissfully mouth-watering experience concluded with a softly-spoken announcement that the foregoing 'thirty seconds of darkness was brought to you by Guinness'.

In the seventies, Guinness posters in Ireland featured strong photographic images with slogans whose ingenuity rivalled that of J. Walter Thompson: 'Familiarity breeds content' and 'Dark fantastic'. Sometimes, however, they were just irritatingly smart.

Perhaps as a reaction against the over-clever puns that had been appearing throughout the seventies, posters at the end of the decade began, instead, to use simple, popular imagery and slogans that were aimed at showing Guinness as a convivial drink for the younger drinker.

Topicality has always been a feature of some of the most successful Guinness advertising. Like their colleagues in the UK, Arks have produced some inspired examples of the topical advertisement – particularly during the short, but worrying, time in 1974 when the Brewery in Dublin was on strike.

Arks's television campaign developed a variety of new themes throughout the seven-

Left: **Poster produced during the strike at the Dublin brewery in 1974.**
Below left and below: **Two punning posters of 1974.**

ties, beginning with 'You're at home with a Guinness'. A foreigner in a Dublin bar asks for directions: 'Scuse, please. Could you direct me to A y-les-bury Road?' 'I know,' says one man. 'You take the first left, right? Then the second left, right?' 'No, no, no!' interrupts

another man. 'You take the second left, right? Then the next right!' 'No, left, right, then over the bridge.' 'Look, if I was you, I wouldn't start here at all.' 'Wherever you go,' says the commentator, 'you're at home with a Guinness.' The bemused foreigner adopts a look of resignation. 'I think I'll stay here, instead.'

A multi-award-winning cinema commercial made in 1977 showed a small West of Ireland bar crowded with people waiting in silent expectation. A clock on the mantel ticks sonorously, and a dog looks anxiously up from beneath one of the bar-stools. The scene

Posters: (*clockwise*) 1979, 1976, 1976, 1981 and 1982.

191

Scenes from the
award-winning cinema
commercial, 'Island' (1977).

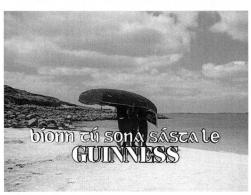

changes to a seascape and we notice a small row-boat approaching the shore. The boat lands and the rowers, shouldering crates of Guinness, make their way up the cliff path to the pub. In the bar, silence reigns until the moment the door opens, the beer is delivered, and the first Guinness is poured, whereupon everyone begins talking at once – in Irish.

Between 1978 and 1981, the theme of the Irish TV commercials became 'Have a Guinness tonight' – which combined lively music with imaginatively shot and edited visuals, in an attempt to present Guinness as a specifically celebratory drink. 'What's a Guinness between friends?' asks the narrator on these commercials. The answer: 'It's when you hit the jackpot and you hear that welcome sound; it's when you get a special deal and really go to town; it's the calm that comes at evening and the sun sets in the west; it's when you play your heart out and the man says you're the best; ... it's when you make it to the top and

Scenes from 'Have a
Guinness Tonight' (1978).

Cinema commercial
'Surfing' (1982), a theme also
used for a poster design (*see
opposite page*).

you're taking in the view, or get the wrong connection and a date with someone new.'

Although these romantic commercials appeared to present Guinness as an inaccessible luxury that had little to do with the experience of most Irish drinkers, the campaign was considered to be one of the most successful ever devised. A Guinness between friends, ran another commercial, is 'when the horse you fancied strides ahead to win the day; a trip in Concorde taking off to New York, USA; it's when you get a lucky break and strike oil in Algeria; like finding it's your birthday with a diamond in your cereal . . .'

In 1981, the advertising campaign invited non-Guinness drinkers to 'move over' to Guinness. And this time, in place of diamonds, racehorses and trips in Concorde, the new commercials featured the special contents and qualities of Guinness.

A new departure from Guinness advertising in Ireland – and generally – began in October 1982 with a series of television commercials and press advertisements, featuring testimonials from various personalities popular in Ireland. Pop singers, footballers, international cyclists, with one thing in common – they all really had to be Guinness drinkers. One of the personalities used, singer Elkie Brooks, had been featured some years earlier, when she was less established, in a Thompson advertisement in the United Kingdom. 'Two things,' says Miss Brooks in her later commercial, 'come very naturally to me: singing the Blues – and sinking a Guinness!' Other testimonials were provided by the ever-popular folk group, the Chieftains; footballer, Frank Stapleton; cyclist, Sean Kelly; tennis-player, Matt Doyle, and musician, Mike Oldfield.

The main slogan for Irish advertising during the 1980s has been 'No beer comes near'. This, as the chief executive of Guinness has said, is 'a recognition that Guinness is not just a dark beer, not just a substitute for lager or bitter – but a truly unique drink.' Uniquely advertised. Like the poster, produced in 1982, of a surf-rider skimming along on the crest of a wave that appeared to be the creamy head of a glass of Guinness.

In what amounts to a little over a decade, the advertising designed for Guinness by Arks has embraced almost every mood and style, whilst at the same time always being very Irish and very Guinness.

Above: **Poster (1980).**
Right: **Press advertisement (1970).**
Far right: **Magazine advertisement featuring the Chieftains (1982).**

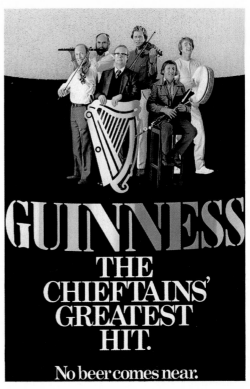

ס'איז נישא
קיין בעסערס
ווי א גינעס

18
ALL THE WORLD OVER

Despite having, as someone has remarked, a name half the world can't spell and the other half can't pronounce, Guinness is sold in over one hundred and fifty countries around the world. It is, of course, spelt and pronounced differently – in some countries it is known by other names – but the international market for Guinness continues to grow and flourish.

Subsidiary companies of Guinness Overseas Ltd operate breweries in Jamaica, Ghana, Nigeria, Cameroon and Malaysia. And Guinness is additionally brewed, under contract, in about fourteen overseas breweries in Australia, New Zealand, Canada, Mauritius, Thailand, Seychelles, Liberia, Sierra Leone, Venezuela and several other countries.

In all these far away places with strange sounding names, posters, press advertisements, television, radio and cinema commercials tell the same story in a dozen different

All the world over

GUINNESS
is good for you

Opposite: **Poster, Cameroon, West Africa (1979). Hebrew advertisement used for Jewish publications in the UK (c 1930).**

languages. The story is simply this: every day, over seven million glasses of Guinness are drunk throughout the world; and people drink it because it's good for them and gives them strength.

In this chapter we will take a round-the-world trip, seeing how some of those seven million glasses of Guinness are advertised.

We will begin our tour in Europe where, as we saw earlier, Guinness was known as long ago as 1815, the year of the Battle of Waterloo. For the most part, European Guinness is brewed in Dublin and shipped to Guinness Exports at Liverpool who arrange for its transportation to the different European agents responsible for bottling and canning the beer.

The longest-standing contract is with John Martin Ltd of Antwerp, who have been importing Guinness into Belgium since 1911. Today, Guinness is still very much in the public eye with the Brewery's sponsorship of rugby football, sailing, rowing and wood-chopping contests. Like so much Guinness advertising overseas, the main slogan used in Belgium is 'Guinness is good for you', with which they have achieved almost national awareness of the drink.

Although France is primarily a wine-drinking nation, its beer consumption has steadily increased over the last decade or so, with specific areas – Paris, Lyon, Lille and the Region D'Alsace – where beer generally, and Guinness in particular, has a devoted following. Although Guinness have not advertised extensively in France, what advertising there has been, has concentrated chiefly on the appeal of Guinness to the connoisseur.

Similar market conditions to those in France exist in Italy, where Guinness is presented as a drink of special character with famous Irish-Anglo origins and associations.

In Germany there is no problem about per-suading people to drink beer – they have the highest per capita beer consumption anywhere in the world! For many years the problem was persuading them to drink Guinness, which had only a very small share of a huge market. Now, however, Germany is the largest market for Guinness on the Continent; and sales are still rising.

Despite its strongly consolidated image on the Continent – a uniformity of appearance not dissimilar to that devised for Guinness in the United Kingdom during the sixties – Guinness's future in Europe presents the Brewery with one of its greatest challenges, and a great deal of potential.

Probably the most successful area for Guinness marketing overseas has been the African continent.

A Guinness brewery was opened in Nigeria in 1963 and, despite expansion, demand still exceeds supply. There, as in much of the rest

Overseas posters: (*top left and left*) Cameroon, West Africa (1980 and 1982); (*above*) General poster used in the early 1970s.

of Africa, the main advertising slogan has, for many years, been 'Guinness for Power' which, by implication, endorses its legendary reputation for virility enhancement.

This slogan has been reproduced on glasses, pens, lighters, key-fobs, bottle-openers, T-shirts and draught boards.

Despite its popularity, a feeling grew up that 'Guinness for Power' placed an unnecessary limitation on where, when and how much Guinness could be drunk. As a result, the advertising now maintains the myth and magic of the Guinness image while attempting to broaden its appeal as a social drink that can be enjoyed by all ages of drinker and by women as well as men.

In Cameroon, the message has become simplified to its quintessence – 'It's the best!' The visual emphasis, as with all the African advertising, is on good-looking, hard-working men who enjoy Guinness and are strengthened by it.

Cinema advertising in Cameroon has adopted a theme reminiscent of Benson's 'There's a whole world in a glass of Guinness'. Here, however, the effect is dynamic with word and image uniting to impress the viewer with the positive qualities of Guinness: 'Guinness has Power' (illustrated by a racing car or speedboat), 'Guinness is Strong' (weightlifter/leopard), 'Guinness is Cool' (polar bear/waterfall), 'Guinness is Friendly' (a pretty girl).

The use of some of these symbols – the driving racing-car, the thrusting speedboat – endorses the image of Guinness as a virility-booster, as do poster captions like 'Discover the secret' and 'Share the secret'.

What is the secret? That Guinness is an enjoyable drink – or that Guinness is a powerful aphrodisiac? The answer is left to the imagination, as is the meaning behind that similarly ambiguous slogan: 'Guinness keeps you on top.'

In the Far East, Guinness is known in a variety of guises. When the beer was first exported to Malaysia, it was decided to provide it with a simple means of identification for the benefit of those who couldn't read English or pronounce the curious name. Each of the companies bottling Guinness adopted a device featuring an animal head, and neck-labels (known as 'chops') were used in addition to the traditional Guinness label.

The Bulldog (Chuan Cow) was bottled by Messrs Guthrie; the Dog's Head (Oho Cow) by Messrs Sime Darby; and the Wolf (Ang Chee Cow, or Red-tongued dog) by Messrs McAlister. Although the brew is the same in each of these bottles, many people in Malaysia will only drink one particular brand, believing it to be demonstrably superior to the others!

Bulldog Guinness was the subject of the earliest recorded overseas press advertisement for Guinness which appeared in *The Malay Mail* in 1908 (below).

Early Malaysian advertising featured the animals used in these brand names. 'This beautiful creature,' began one cinema commercial, 'is a wolf.' A picture of a wolf was then followed by that of a man whistling after an attractive girl. 'Another wolf! There are all kinds of wolves in the world, but only one Wolf Stout! Guinness Wolf Stout! Guinness for Strength! A world-famous saying and a well-known fact. Guinness Wolf Stout, famous ACROSS THE WORLD!'

So well-known a fact is 'Guinness for

Far left: **American bar-mirror (1967).**
Left: **Australian show-card (1968).**
Below: **Lapel badges, Cameroons (1968).**

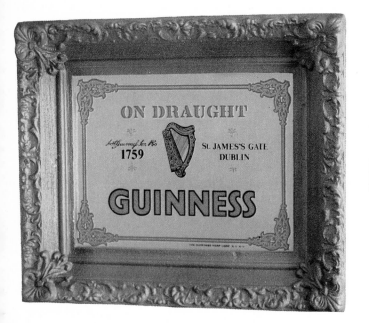

Strength' that in many far eastern countries it is customary to bathe a new-born baby in Guinness believing this to have a beneficial effect on the child.

Another commercial featured a conjurer who takes a model of a bull and a model of a dog, and 'Hey presto!' turns them into a Guinness Bulldog. 'This is the best way to make it disappear,' says the conjurer, drinking it down, 'and you don't need to be a magician. Doctors agree, Guinness is good for inducing healthy sleep, as a tonic after illness and during pregnancy. For extra energy, vitality and strength, drink Bulldog Bottled Guinness every day.' We see the conjurer then settle down for a good night's sleep.

'All animal lovers,' began another of these commercials, 'enjoy a good dog-show, and this one is the event of the year. The winner will receive a trophy and be garlanded with laurel leaves. Will it be the boxer? Or the Alsatian? Or the pom? Or the dachshund? This is a difficult task for the judges. Maybe it will be the Pekinese – but the judges have finally decided on the winner! And the winner is Bulldog Bottled Guinness – everyone's favourite!'

Since these early advertisements, a greater sophistication has been adopted: to begin with, current commercials, not unreasonably, are featuring people drinking Guinness as opposed to dog-shows and conjuring-acts; and an attempt is being made to advertise Guinness as a brand name rather than the old familiar 'chop' brands. Guinness Stout does, however, have its own phonetic spelling in Malaysia – Ginis Setaut!

Malaysian Guinness commercials depict hard-working men – truck-drivers, bridge-builders, loggers and miners – successfully overcoming the difficulties and challenges of their jobs, and then enjoying the reward of a Guinness after work. The theme is a familiar one, as is the signature tune which was first used twenty years ago in Benson's 'End of the day' commercials.

In Singapore, similar visuals are accompanied by this highly emotive description of a Guinness drinker:

'He's a man who knows the feeling. He's a man who knows the score. Who'd never dream of giving up, no matter what's in store. You couldn't help but notice, you couldn't help but see. He's proud and he's a winner, and he's proud because he's free. He's a man who's never lonely. Any man would call him "friend". He'll never change – he'll *never change* – *he's a real man among men.*'

A series of commercials for Hong Kong shows craftsmen making neon-signs and printing posters. At the end of each film, their work done, they settle down to enjoy a Guinness and we see that the neon-sign or the poster they were making, advertises – Guinness.

In complete contrast to the hustle and bustle of life reflected in the Hong Kong commercials, a film for Thailand shows a very different life-style. A solitary fisherman at sea enjoys a glass of Guinness while waiting for his catch. What is curious is that he should have an elegant Guinness goblet from which to drink it!

In Australia, TV advertising has tended to take a somewhat idiosyncratic look at the odd characteristics of Guinness:

'So – you're about to try your first Guinness? It's going to be a bit bitter – but you can handle that! Funny colour – black an' all, but look at that creamy head. Come on – there's nothing to it! Guinness. Try one – at least once!'

In the late sixties, an organisation called the G-Men Club was formed to encourage the drinking of Guinness. It had badges, membership cards and chains of office decorated with bottle-tops. It was not a success!

Obviously the man used to thinking of beer in terms of a tube of Fosters needs something a little less gimicky to get him to try a funny-coloured beer like Guinness. One attempt opted for a more sophisticated – even cultural – approach. A pint of Draught Guinness was shown being drawn to the sound of Bach's Toccata and Fugue in D Minor:

'Draught Guinness is unique.
It's one of the world's great tastes.
True you have to wait for the rich creamy head to separate from the dark, mysteri-

ous depths, but then Guinness has taken two hundred years to get to Australia, so another few seconds won't matter.'

Which prompted one barmaid to ask: 'Do you want a beer while you're waiting?'

In the United States of America, Guinness is a household name – as the proprietor of the famous *Guinness Book of Records*, which has sold more than 30 000 000 copies in the USA and which was recently the subject of a series of glossy documentaries hosted by David Frost. Not everybody realises, however, that the name Guinness is also the name of a beer that was, at one time, brewed on Long Island.

In the Irish bars of New York, of course, Guinness is drunk if not in staggering quantities then certainly with nostalgic enthusiasm. What Guinness advertising for the American market has tended to do in the past is to concentrate on Guinness's Irishness (an aspect which has always been underplayed in the UK). Its view of Ireland, however, is pure whimsy with leprechauns, shamrocks and shillelaghs.

Not that this folksy image of Guinness has been entirely confined to the USA. In 1966, Guinness began producing Leprechaun Charms as give-aways to drinkers in Africa and Asia. Just 1⅛ inches high, he might have been mistaken for Enid Blyton's Big Ears, had it not been for the fact that he was clutching an Irish harp in his left hand. He came pinned to a card with a replica of the Guinness label on it and the words 'Irish Luck from GUINNESS'. A short explanation told recipients that leprechauns were 'renowned in folklore for their impish good influence on the larger species of the human race, being harbingers of good fortune, health and prosperity'. Thousands of Guinness drinkers in Africa and Asia are now available as research subjects to anyone interested in exploring the topic of charm potency...

As a fitting conclusion to this world tour, it is interesting to note that Guinness has established a showy presence for itself in central Florida. Part of Walt Disney World's EPCOT Center (EPCOT being an acronym for Experimental Prototype Community of Tomorrow) is a permanent world's fair attraction called World Showcase. There one can visit a series of pavilions representing different nations that replicate the architectural style and offer traditional merchandise and cuisine from those countries.

The United Kingdom pavilion has an 'authentic London pub', *The Rose & Crown*, sponsored by Guinness and Bass.

In Walt Disney's microcosmic world – as in the larger version – Guinness is being enjoyed for what it is: rewarding, distinctive, unique.

All over the world, life is brighter after a Guinness.

Joni, one of Walt Disney's hostesses at EPCOT Center in Florida, USA, serving a pint of Guinness outside 'The Rose & Crown' (© Walt Disney Productions 1982.)

Breaking soon, the new Guinness campaign.

19

FLY AWAY TOUCAN

In 1979, Guinness celebrated the fiftieth anniversary of Guinness advertising with a major exhibition at the Park Royal Brewery, and the production of a special glass decorated with a stylish portrait of the Guinness toucan.

In Ireland, a poster was produced featuring some of John Gilroy's famous characters, while, in the United Kingdom, an advertisement (opposite) appeared in the trade press, suggesting that the gentleman who had asked Guinness to bring back the animals was about to have his wish granted.

That hatching toucan caused more than a few raised eyebrows in the advertising industry. After all, Guinness had gone through traumas to rid itself of the toucan and all it represented. Now, twenty years later, it looked as if the bird was set to return.

Alec Morrison, Guinness account director at J. Walter Thompson, explained the decision to *Campaign*: 'The brand is so big and strong,' he said, 'that when we discussed a specific take-home promotion we were looking for something outside the main stream – Guinness in the home, not the pub.'

At the time, Britain's off-trade was outgrowing the on-trade six-to-one and Guinness wanted to get an increasing share of that expanding business. They faced, however, the

Opposite: **Trade advertisement (1979).**
Below: **Glasses issued to celebrate the Golden Jubilee of Guinness advertising (1979).**

recurrent problem of getting the public to understand when an advertisement was intended to promote a particular aspect of the product rather than being merely a general advertisement for Guinness. A few years earlier, in 1976, just such an attempt had been made, using television comedians, Peter Cook and Dudley Moore, in a not very successful promotion for take-home Guinness.

One of the Pete and Dud television commercials began with an opening shot of three Guinness bottles mounted on plinths with inscription plates. Pete's hand comes in and lifts out one of these bottles, and handling it carefully – like a trophy – he walks towards the camera. Three candles are seen in the foreground and, as the camera pulls back, we discover Dud seated at the table, and notice that the candle-holders are Guinness bottles in the shape of a candelabrum. Pete sits at the table and chats to Dud, who is relentlessly tucking into his food whilst Pete reminisces:

PETE: You know, this is one Guinness I'll never forget, Dud.

DUD: Oh, it's empty, Pete.

PETE: How would I never forget it, if I hadn't drunk it?

DUD: Oh, yeah!

PETE: Sausage, eggs, chips, beans and gravy.

DUD: Hold on. Shirley Powell.

PETE: Who else!

DUD: Ah yes!

PETE: A culinary tone-poem.

DUD: A what?

PETE: Washed down with a Guinness that only can be described as perfection. Cool, dry, slightly bitter.

DUD: Bitter.

PETE: Perfectly off-setting Shirley's . . . er . . . immaculate baked beans. An unforgettable repast, Dud.

DUD: An unforgettable girl, Pete!

PETE: Truly unforgettable.

DUD: When was this unforgettable repast?

PETE: I forget, Dud.

For the new campaign, in 1979, it was decided that the toucan might fit the bill. The bird was thought to be naturally suited to work for Guinness, whether or not the public were aware of its earlier association with the product. 'They are extremely elegant and personable birds,' says David Holmes, who worked on the campaign. 'They are a bit black and white, and they are redolent of the Guinness values. They also behave in a Guinnessy sort of way!'

In the difficult business of advertising, where it can sometimes prove fatal to assume that the public understands anything which has not just been explained to them, Guinness were attempting a tricky manoeuvre. The toucan campaign was intended to revive memories of yesterday without appearing to be speaking with yesterday's voice. 'The new toucan,' said Alec Morrison, 'is totally different, but is within the framework of Guinness promotions.'

'If the toucan had not existed,' says David Holmes, 'it would have been necessary to have invented something as powerful, despite the fact that it wouldn't have had a heritage of any sort.' The heritage that did exist consisted of artwork and animated cartoons, but it was now decided that the toucan's new commercials would be filmed as live-action, and that the

bird would be seen as a tame, household pet.

The search for a performing toucan led eventually to Stephen Edgington's pet centre in Hassocks, near Brighton, where Thompsons found Tookie, a natural who did everything but talk. However, since he was going to *have* to talk, the next task was to find him a suitable voice. That took a little longer and, among those who were tested for the part, were Peter Cook and animal-impersonator, Percy Edwards. The part finally went to Anton Rodgers, who intuitively knew how a toucan would talk if a toucan could.

The first commercial was appropriately entitled 'Talking Lesson,' and the toucan was seen listening to the sound of a ring being pulled on a can of drink. 'Next time the wife goes shopping,' says the toucan's owner, 'I want you to say "Don't forget the Guinness".' He repeats the words to the toucan, who listens attentively. 'Don't forget the Guinness. Don't forget the Guinness. Don't forget the Guinness.' At which point, the door opens and the wife comes in. The bird looks at her as she enters the room and calls out to her: 'Hello, Mrs Lovell, bad news, I'm afraid – your husband's turning into a parrot!'

In the next commercial, the wife returns after a few days away. 'Hello, love,' she says, as she comes in. 'Me Mum sends her love. Fixed

Trade advertisement announcing the televising of the new toucan commercials during breaks in ITV's *Coronation Street*.

THE ROVERS RETURN.

You could probably do with a Guinness tonight.

Above: TV Times
advertisement produced in 1981 to coincide with the first screening on TV of Jaws.
Right: **Press advertisement introducing Toucan Tokens (1979).**
Below: **Poster, January 1982.**

50ᴾ OFF YOUR NEXT BILL.

All you've got to do is collect a dozen Toucan Tokens from special-offer cans of Guinness, or packs of no-deposit bottles at your supermarket or off-licence. Just look for the packs with the toucan on.

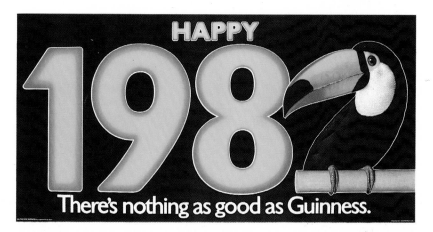

HAPPY 1982
There's nothing as good as Guinness.

the window then for me, did you?' The husband looks around guiltily. 'Mended the table?' asks the wife. The toucan, on his perch, looks and listens with interest. 'I hope you've been getting a few early nights in while I've been away,' she continues, 'instead of having all your mates round every evening?' 'Course not,' replies the husband, and, turning to the toucan for corroboration, adds, 'We were all on our own, weren't we?' The toucan nods. The husband then quickly changes the subject, asking his wife: 'Do you fancy a Guinness?' Before she can reply, the toucan begins to chatter away nineteen-to-the-dozen. 'Hello, Tom. Fancy a Guinness? Hello, David. Fancy a Guinness? Come in, Harry. Fancy a Guinness? Hello, Nigel. Fancy a Guinness? Hello, Fred. Fancy a Guinness? . . .'

Probably the best remembered of the toucan commercials is that in which his owner is seen attempting to convince a friend that the bird can talk. 'Watch this,' he says. 'What's this I'm drinking?' 'Guinness,' replies the toucan. 'And what's this that John's drinking?' 'Guinness.' 'And what's this I'm pouring out for Jenny?' 'Guinness.' The man smiles proudly and takes the drink out of the room to give to his wife. 'Right, then,' says the friend, now alone with the bird. 'Who won the F.A. Cup in 1958?' The toucan is silent and the young man returns to his drink with a smug look on his face. But, just as he takes his first sip, the toucan answers: 'Bolton Wanderers!'

There was a huge supporting campaign for the television commercials, with posters, press advertisements and money-saving toucan-tokens on take-home packs of Guinness.

The campaign was extended to radio:

1ST VOICE: In the Guinness story that follows, the toucan performs many death-defying stunts. Listeners are warned, therefore, not to try to imitate him.

2ND VOICE: Gunning his sleek orange beak through the damp stillness of the Essex evening, secret agent Double-O-Toucan hurtled homeward to London.
But danger still lurked in the wings, for he was carrying a precious cargo of Guinness.
Suddenly, agents from THRUSH were after the Guinness.
Double-O-Toucan slewed to the left with a screech of burning claws and made good his escape.

1ST VOICE: A close shave.

2ND VOICE: He said,

1ST VOICE: Water off a duck's back.

2ND VOICE: He added, sardonically. He decided the moment he got home he would treat himself to some vintage bird seed.
And, of course, a can of Guinness – not shaken, not stirred.

1ST VOICE: Are *you* going home to a Guinness?

This was followed by another witty advertisement on the same bird-brained theme:

1ST VOICE: The Guinness story that follows, 'The Maltese Toucan', is true. Ish. Only the beaks have been changed, to protect the innocent.

2ND VOICE: It was a cold November night and I was just another rookie on his way home, arms cradling a pack of Guinness like it was my favourite dame.
It was raining cats and dogs, with the occasional – mystery guest.

TOUCAN: Toucan!

2ND VOICE: Suddenly my size tens connected with a wet banana and my Guinness went the wrong way down a one-way street.
I thought it was curtains, then, out of the blue swooped this dude!

TOUCAN: Geronimo!

2ND VOICE: He looked like Schnozzle Durante, only orange. He saved my Guinness before it bit the sidewalk, and I thanked him from the bottom of my wallet.

TOUCAN: Don't mention it.

2ND VOICE: He said. But I will. Guinness.

1ST VOICE: Are *you* going home to Guinness?

In September 1979, Thompsons pulled off one of the best free publicity campaigns ever perpetrated.

It began with an attempt to provide Guinness with a little publicity on the tenth anniversary of their association with JWT. It was going to be reported that the toucan had escaped. The story was going to be kept alive until the evening of a dinner which Thompsons were giving in Guinness's honour, when the bird would be found nesting in one of the trees in Berkeley Square.

The toucan's keeper, Stephen Edgington, told the *Evening Argus* and, within a couple of days, in the words of Alec Morrison, 'All hell broke loose!' Every daily newspaper was reporting the story – with quite excessive coverage in the popular tabloids and in the the *Evening Argus*, which was, not unnaturally, making the most of having broken the sensational news.

Guinness, who also supposed the story to be true, offered a reward of one hundred pounds and one hundred cans of Guinness, while Mr Edgington kept the press fed with bogus information and Thompsons began to wonder if the whole thing might suddenly backfire on them. Eventually, they decided to announce that the toucan had been 'found' – somebody, reputedly, having spotted him in a tree in Sussex and rung Edgington's shop. The identity of the toucan-finder had, of course, to remain a mystery, even in the face of the *Argus* wanting to run a campaign to discover the identity of this public-spirited citizen and present him with his reward.

In October 1981, the toucan gave a particularly affecting performance in a colour advertisement, specially designed for *TV Times*, on the first television screening of *Jaws*.

A rather different toucan from that originally conceived by Dorothy L. Sayers and John Gilroy, but the fun and games made it seem quite like old times.

The irony of the toucan's continued success was that what began as a special campaign limited to promoting sales of take-home Guinness, grew and grew until the bird was

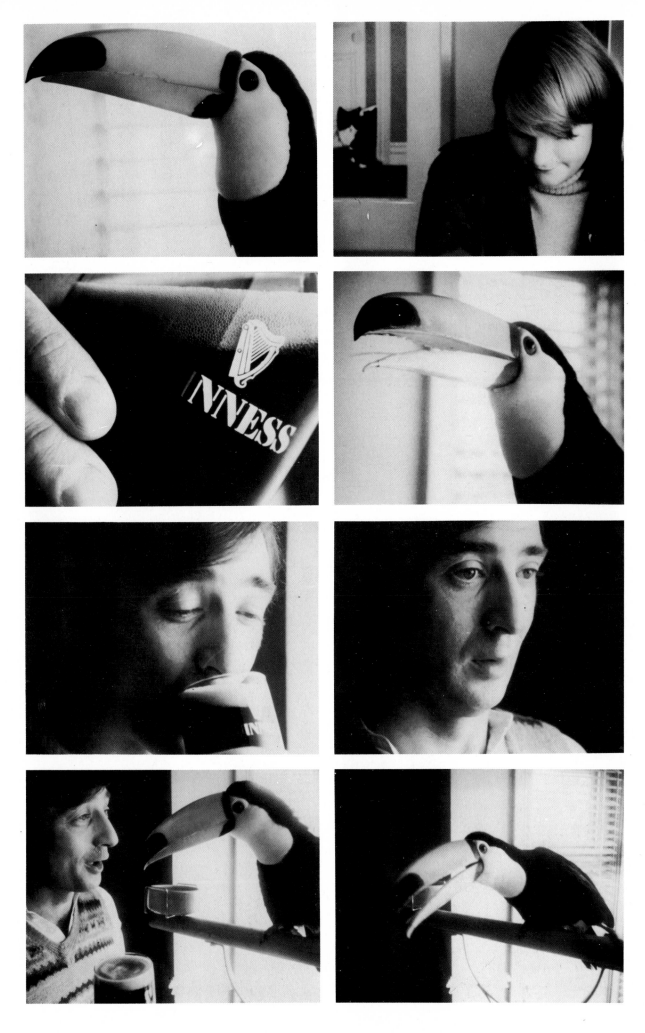

eventually spearheading the advertising for the main Guinness product.

In the winter of 1981, the Guinness toucans suddenly and mysteriously appeared to have begun migration. Perhaps they knew something about Guinness advertising that Thompsons didn't know.

On New Year's Eve, a TV commercial appeared, showing the toucan popping out of Big Ben like a cuckoo-clock: 'Guinness would like to wish everyone all the very best in nineteen eighty . . . toucan.'

In the twelve years since Thompsons had inherited the Guinness advertising account from S. H. Benson, they had succeeded in preserving the qualities that had made Guinness advertisements so universally beloved, while, at the same time, giving it a style and sophistication it had never previously possessed. But, despite their efforts to make Guinness a more accessible drink to those who had never tried it, Guinness faced very serious problems with sales-figures falling and some people prophesying that the Company was in a state of terminal decline.

For J. Walter Thompson it was not going to be a very happy nineteen-eighty-toucan. The Guinness Board appointed a new chief executive in Ernest Saunders, who had new ideas about the Guinness product and about the Guinness advertising.

Right: **Poster (1981).**
Below: **'Nineteen Eighty-Toucan', scenes from a TV commercial produced for New Year's Eve, 1981.**

20

GUINNLESS WONDERS

O n 15 January 1982, a curious headline appeared on the front page of *Campaign*, the advertising industry's newspaper: 'GUINNESS SET TO QUIT JWT?' The question-mark suggested uncertainty – or, possibly, incredulity – for it was the first intimation that the twelve-year association between Guinness and J. Walter Thompson might be at an end. The uncertainty and incredulity were understandable. Guinness was very much regarded as an establishment company, and this was reflected in its advertising and its use of an establishment agency like Thompsons. *Campaign*'s report went on to suggest that Guinness's UK advertising account was about to be transferred to the company of Allen, Brady & Marsh Ltd.

Opposite: **Peter Marsh and Rod Allen posing for a trade advertisement with their Guinnless poster. Friends of the Guinnless logo.** *This page:* **ABM finally silence the famous toucan.**

Despite a frantic flurry of enquiries by journalists, little could be discovered; then, after a week of fevered anticipation, an official announcement confirmed that the account had indeed passed from JWT to ABM. In an interview with the *Financial Times*, Ernest Saunders, the new chief executive of Guinness, explained the decision: 'My task,' he said, 'is to take a totally professional look at the business, and advertising – even at Guinness – is not just an art form, but a vital part of communications and business strategy. We need a totally fresh look at the advertising question, and we need a new agency to do the job.'

That agency was the all-British, privately-owned and rapidly expanding company of Allen, Brady & Marsh, an agency with a self-styled reputation for 'voice-of-the-people advertising'. Within the industry, ABM had become famous not only for its exceptionally intrusive campaigns, but also its ability to give long-standing brands new relevance for the consumer.

Founded in 1966, ABM was a comparatively young agency, although acquiring the Guinness account placed them as the fifth largest advertising agency in Britain. Among their accounts, for whom they had devised compelling catchphrases and jolly jingles, were R. Whites lemonade, British Rail, Midland Bank, Weetabix and The National Milk Publicity Council. From March 1980, they had also handled the partly Guinness-owned Harp Lager account ('Harp stays sharp to the bottom of the glass').

ABM's success was the result of a partnership between two men with creative flair and entrepreneurial insight – Rod Allen and Peter Marsh, although it is invariably the latter who provides the public focus of attention for the agency. Becoming chairman of ABM in 1974, Peter Marsh established himself as an extravagant and outspoken personality and media pundit which had the consistent effect of bringing publicity, and clients, to ABM.

Whilst it would be difficult to imagine an advertising agency more different from S. H. Benson than ABM, there is much about Mr Marsh that recalls Bobby Bevan, the 'bobby-dazzler' of post-war advertising at Bensons. A forceful, determined and ambitious man, his philosophy of advertising is displayed (with the reverence given to icons) on the walls of his elegant offices, and published in a glossy booklet modestly entitled *The Pursuit of Excellence*.

'We believe,' runs one of his articles of faith, 'in the hard work ethic. Hard work and consistent application pursued intelligently will always produce results.' They also believe in 'flair, talent, the spirit of the entrepreneur and the unplanned, unco-ordinated wisdom of the market place'.

It was this credo that attracted the Guinness management, plus the agency's record in

209

handling the Harp Lager account and glowing testimonials from delighted clients.

ABM joyfully celebrated winning the Guinness account with an advertisement in the trade press which parodied Gilroy's famous 'Weathervane' poster from the 1950s.

Clearly Messrs Marsh and Allen were in no doubt as to which way the wind was blowing at Guinness. Soon, they were back down to earth and busily working on the new Guinness campaign in total secrecy. 'Our security,' said Peter Marsh, 'would make Trappist monks look like a lot of chatterboxes!' The hounds of Fleet Street couldn't get so much as a scent of what was going on, and when, in June 1982, a new Guinness poster appeared, many people supposed it marked the beginning of ABM's campaign, and were somewhat surprised to find that it had a toucan on it.

Produced to commemorate the birth of Prince William of Wales, and given the warm approval of the Royal Press Secretary, it was actually the last Guinness poster to be designed by J. Walter Thompson.

A few months later, Thompsons used the famous bird again – or, rather, its absence – to announce to the trade the number of new accounts which the agency had won since the departure of Guinness. Showing an empty bird-cage with an open door and a few stray black feathers fluttering by, it was simply captioned: 'Even losing Guinness is good for you.'

A toucan sang in Berkeley Square no longer, and Peter Marsh's comment that toucans have nothing to do with selling Guinness, suggested that it might not be encouraged to roost on the roof of ABM House. There, the agency's creative team was still engaged on what was sub-sequently claimed to be 'the most researched, most thoroughly thought-out campaign in the history of British advertising'.

ABM determined that Guinness should have an image which would firmly establish the drink 'as part of today's pub culture'. In the past, Guinness directed their advertising to all sectors of the population, from readers of *The Tatler* to readers of *The Sun*. Now, in more competitive times, it was decided, at least in the short term, to concentrate the advertising on the target audience with the greatest potential to increase volume sales. Specifically, the need was to promote Guinness to the younger, heavier-drinking sector. In recent years, they had been wooed to the more fashionable lagers, and the job for the new advertising was to win young drinkers over to Guinness.

That target audience was finally pinpointed as twenty-four to thirty-four-year-old men in the socio-economic group defined as C2DE. Among this group – which represents 71 per cent of all beer drinkers – were a great many men who drank Guinness only occasionally; ABM decided to challenge them to drink it rather more frequently. 'What we had to do,' says Peter Marsh, 'was plug into attitudes common to beer drinkers and make ordering a pint of Guinness a desirable thing to do.'

This plan of campaign corresponded exactly with the aims of Ernest Saunders. However, some observers thought that if drinking trends had turned so dramatically away from stout there was no way in which that trend could be stopped – let alone reversed – by advertising. ABM did not accept that argument and began searching for an approach.

Within its creative department, seven poss-

J. Walter Thompson's last Guinness poster, celebrating the birth of Prince William of Wales (June 1982).

ible campaigns were masterminded, each with fully developed designs for posters and detailed story-boards for television commercials. Every one of these potential campaigns had to meet a rigorous, and sometimes paradoxical, series of demands. For example, whilst Guinness was to be presented as a 'normal beer' that might be enjoyed by anyone, it had also to be seen as a 'unique beer'.

Following exhaustive consumer-testing, one campaign emerged as the winner. It was to feature the 'Guinnless', people who had gone too long between one Guinness and the next, or even worse, were going through life without even trying Guinness. To help them on to the path of endarkenment, a fictitious organisation was created called 'Friends of the Guinnless'. The Guinnless idea, says Peter Marsh, 'enabled us to express the virtues of the brand in a way that the potential user would not find off-putting.' The campaign was budgeted at £7 million.

The British public first became aware of the existence of the Guinnless when, in January 1983, a poster appeared on a thousand hoardings up and down the country. It caused an immediate sensation (and almost resulted in the present writer stepping under an oncoming bus at Fulham Broadway!). Produced in the style and colours of the early Gilroy posters, it showed an empty glass with the legend: 'Guinnless isn't good for you.'

Some people (including the publican's periodical, the *Morning Advertiser*) thought it said 'Guinness isn't good for you'; others supposed that it was a spelling error, and hundreds of callers jammed the switchboard at the Park Royal Brewery with puzzled enquiries.

Neither Guinness nor ABM would explain the mystery word, and it was a reporter on the *Pontypridd Observer* who was the first to correctly hazard a guess at its meaning. The linguistics department at Cardiff University College was invited to comment, but was unimpressed. 'It just doesn't sound right,' a spokesman said. 'Perhaps a better word would be Guinnesslessness. There is no such word as Guinn, therefore you can't be Guinnless. There is no structure about the word and I don't think it will ever go into the *Oxford English Dictionary*.'

It was, however, already deeply established in the public's consciousness, and the speed with which it was mimicked and parodied is an indication of the poster's impact.

There were those who wondered why it had taken ABM twelve months simply to add one letter and take away the Guinness from a poster that had first appeared over fifty years before. Others were surprised that the agency that had talked of breaking with tradition, appeared now to be replicating it. However, although a number of other Gilroy parodies had been designed, it was never intended for more than one to be used.

One unexpected response to Guinnlessness came in the form of a protest by the temperance organisation, the United Kingdom Alliance. The Alliance – who felt that people with drinking problems would be better off for being Guinnless – presented their objections to the Advertising Standards Authority, arguing that the phrase 'Guinnless isn't good for you' was a tautology for 'Guinness *is* good for you' – a slogan which it was thought would not be allowable under the terms of the present advertising code. This new controversy generated even more publicity, with much media speculation about whether the £7 million campaign would have to be abandoned.

Trade advertisement imitating Gilroy's famous weather vane poster.

Preliminary designs for Guinnless posters – none of which made it on to the hoardings, but one of which features yet a further adaptation of Gilroy's girder-carrier.

"Seven million quid of advertising ruined at a stroke."

The Guinnless campaign quickly inspired the cartoonists of Fleet Street to some topical jokes. These two are by David Langdon (*right*) and Mahood (*below*). *Overleaf:* One of the first striking poster designs used by ABM.

The Advertising Standards Authority considered the complaint, but decided they could not support the semantic argument put forward. 'The Authority did not accept,' said their report, 'that to say "Guinnless isn't good for you" was logically equivalent to saying "Guinness is good for you". They did not believe it likely that the public would understand the poster in that sense, or as asserting that "Guinnlessness" was necessarily undesirable for all.'

In the pages of *Campaign*, Guinness took space to make 'An Important Announcement':

> After protracted discussion with our agency, Allen, Brady and Marsh, we have decided that there will be no Guinness Advertising in 1983 ... After months of soul-searching and heart-rending, we have decided to put our money to better use helping the Guinnless ...

The controversial first poster was followed by designs that ranged from the simple directness of 'Relief for the Guinnless' with its bold lettering and prominent display of the product, to the detailed fine art featured on the 'Centres for the Guinnless' poster. Another poster featured an L-plated cocktail in the midst of a row of Guinness glasses.

Guinness addicts and converts were soon to be seen sporting Friends of the Guinnless ties, T-shirts and sweat shirts, or popping into off-licences with their Guinnless carrier-bags.

A press campaign highlighted the different symptoms of Guinnlessness, commercial radio had a spoof phone-in programme offering advice to the Guinnless, and television carried a series of reports on the malaise and its treatment – after suitable warnings in the press for those of a nervous disposition:

A WARNING TO LONDON WEEK-END TELEVISION VIEWERS

Tonight LWT will be screening a series of public information films on behalf of Friends of the Guinnless. These will feature explicit scenes of Guinnlessness and may prove disturbing to regular Guinness drinkers.

In 1983 Britain enjoyed what turned out to be the hottest summer on record. It was in this unusually hot weather that Guinness launched its summer campaign with a new poster and television commercial. The film featured John Wells, who impersonated David Attenborough exploring the sun-drenched beaches of Skegness in search of the Guinnless.

As this was 'the silly season', the newspapers and BBC TV's Breakfast Time were quick to investigate a rumour that the setting for the new commercial was not, in fact, Skegness but Weymouth. Breakfast Time interviewed Peter Marsh and showed the entire commercial free.

Although the people of Skegness felt that Mr Wells should have visited their beaches, they were none the less pleased with the free publicity. Weymouth, however, was less happy, and the town's hoteliers threatened to stop selling Guinness. An ambassador from

Relief for th

**Issued by
Friends of the Guinnless**

Centres for the Guinn

ERIC: Could I have a Guinness love? Make mine a Guinness. . . .

PRESENTER: We spend a lot of our time working with the Guinnless. People like Eric here who, through simple neglect, have let the word Guinness slip from their

ordering vocabulary.
ERIC: I'll have a Guinness.
PRESENTER: But we believe that Eric is about ready to enjoy life to the full.

ERIC: I'll have a Guinness.
PRESENTER: . . . again

ERIC: I'll have a Guinness. I'll have a . . .
PRESENTER: . . . Guinness
ERIC: I'll have a Guinness.
PRESENTER: Eric, relax. Now, go and order yourself a beautiful, black pint of Guinness.
ERIC: Right I'll have a Guinness. . . .

BARMAID: Hello Eric – the usual?
ERIC: Yeah . . . no.

PRESENTER: Two days later, you'll be pleased to know, Eric successfully ordered a pint of Guinness.

Guinness was despatched to Weymouth on a peace-mission, and was depicted by the cartoonist of the *Daily Star* as being buried up to the neck on Weymouth sands.

The Skegness sand-storm aside, the Guinnless campaign was not without its detractors. Peter Fiddick, television critic of *The Guardian*, described the campaign as 'trite and witless' and went on to add that if Guinness continued with it 'they might find Guinnlessness catching on'. Some people thought Friends of the Guinnless came perilously near making fun of genuine charitable organisations; others thought ABM had made a major miscalculation in tampering with the revered and sacrosanct name of 'Guinness'. For the most part, however, the campaign's critics did not belong to the socio-economic group that ABM had selected as its target audience. The C2DE drinkers themselves gave Friends of the Guinnless the thumbs-up.

Without doubt, ABM had made Guinness more talked about than it had been for years. Within just three months the Guinnless had achieved 87 per cent spontaneous awareness among all adults – including a vicar in Wandsworth who erected a sign outside his church which read: 'Godless Isn't Good For You'!

The friends of the Guinnless had successfully achieved the short-term objectives and had revitalised the position of Guinness in the beer market as well as giving it a new image to attract the younger drinker.

In 1984, Guinness decided that the foundations had been laid for a longer term campaign. As soon as it was known that Guinness was in the market for a new style of advertising, over eighty companies applied for the job of supplying it. Eventually, the choice was narrowed down to just two agencies: Allen, Brady & Marsh and Ogilvy & Mather (who already handled Guinness advertising internationally). Both agencies were given a closely defined brief, which has itself become famous in the industry. The agency chosen was Ogilvy & Mather.

Ogilvy & Mather was founded in New York, in 1949, by David Ogilvy, a man whom *Time* magazine described as 'the most sought-after wizard in the advertising business'.

Today, Ogilvy & Mather is the fourth largest advertising agency in the world, with 185 offices in 41 countries; and Ogilvy himself is generally acknowledged as being one of the major forces responsible for the shaping of post-war advertising.

In 1984, they began handling Guinness's international advertising, but they have had other prior associations with the product in that, in 1971, they took over the advertising agency S. H. Benson who, all those years before, had invented the slogan 'Guinness is

GUINNLESS IS...

HAVING SQUARE EYES

Makes a point of watching the Test Card. And while it's on, he videos the Test Card on the other three channels so he won't miss anything.

In fact, he spends so much time goggling, he's Guinnless. That is, he's well overdue for a deliciously smooth drop of Guinness down at the local.

The best bet is to take him to a pub with a black and white set to make sure he gets the message.

SWITCH OVER TO GUINNESS TONIGHT.

We wish you a Merry Guinness!

ABM's 1983 Christmas poster for Guinness was part of a tradition dating back to 1929. Here are some seasonal greetings from Guinness over the years.

My Goodness My Christmas GUINNESS

The message of Guinnlessness becomes Gospel! (Photo: Judy Goldhill).

good for you'.

David Ogilvy's ideas about advertising are as strong as his predecessors'. 'I do not regard advertising as entertainment or an art form, but as a medium of information. When I write an advertisement, I don't want you to tell me that you find it "creative". I want you to find it so interesting that you buy the product.'

By the time this book is published, Ogilvy & Mather will be hard at work getting you interested enough to drink even more Guinness. In achieving that end, one thing at least is certain – Ogilvy & Mather will be writing a fascinating new chapter in the story of Guinness advertising. . . .

Above: **The Guinnless person depicted as the joker of the pack.** *Right:* **Summer 1983 saw a heat-wave in Britain and this Guinness poster.**

POSTSCRIPT

S ince it always takes a little while for the white-part to separate from the black-part, I've probably got time for a few final thoughts . . .

In beginning this story, I described Guinness advertising as an institution. Institution suggests a vast monolithic structure, incapable of change, demanding admiration by virtue of its sheer size and durability.

But Guinness advertising is an institution, that has constantly developed, progressed and, sometimes, retreated. In each of the five decades of its life, it has displayed a different public face – either from choice or from force of circumstance. Yet every one of these changing faces has become a facet of the Guinness legend, a part of the very institution they may, originally, have seemed to challenge.

Ask anyone who has worked on Guinness advertising what quality it needs to possess, and again and again they will say 'uniqueness', 'oddness', 'quirkiness'. Which, with one or two exceptions (quirky by their very lack of quirkiness!) is what Guinness advertising has always possessed.

The ways in which this quality has been demonstrated are, nevertheless, multifariously different. The first 'Good for You' posters; John Gilroy's girder-carrier et al.; Dorothy Sayers' toucan poem; Ronald Barton and Bobby Bevan's *Alice* parodies; H. M. Bateman's war-time cartoons; Lewitt-Him's Guinness Clock; Stanley Penn's puns; John Trench's verses; Halas and Batchelor's cartoon commercials; Bruce Hobbs's type-face; J. Walter Thompson's talking toucan; and ABM's Friends of the Guinnless.

All are part of the institution, yet all resulted from facing the challenge of commercial, economic and social changes. The Depression, the war-years, the post-war recession, the adoption of market-research, the birth of the television age, the increase and diversity of competition – all these factors have contributed to building, extending, pulling down and restoring that institution. That has been the case ever since 1927, when the Guinness Board first faced the challenge of advertising.

In the years ahead, many more challenges and changes will, doubtless, have to be faced. But whatever happens, Guinness Advertising will always retain a uniquely Guinnessy quality that one might call – GUINNESSNESS.

That's something worth drinking to.

In this previously unpublished Gilroy portrait, the zoo keeper raises his glass to the future of Guinness advertising.

Every year, from 1933 to 1966 (with a short interruption during the War), Guinness produced a Christmas booklet to entertain their friends in the medical profession.

These booklets have now become much sought after by collectors of works illustrated by such artists as Ardizzone, Emett and Whistler and also by Lewis Carroll enthusiasts who have no less than five books based on the Alice stories to collect.

This is the first bibliographical listing of these publications and in compiling it the author is indebted to John Trench for his assistance with identifying the authors of these booklets.

Unless otherwise stated, the format of the books is 9¼in × 6in and printed in full colour.

1a. The Guinness Alice
St James's Gate, Dublin, 1933 pp. 24
[Written by Ronald Barton & Robert Bevan].
Illustrated by John Gilroy
[This First Edition, coded on last page GA281, contains both line and colour illustrations. The contents are as follows: 'A Sane Lunch Party' (col), 'The Walrus and the Carpenter' (b & w), [To the Civilised World it was Guinness that said] (col), [Father William] (b & w), 'A Song to Comfort You' (b & w), '"Off with it's Head!" cried the Queen' (col), 'Maddening!' (b & w), 'Lobster Quadrille' (b & w), ''Tis the Voice of the Lobster' (col), 'The Hunting of the Stout' (b & w), 'Second Sight' (b & w), '"Oh my ears and whiskers!"' (b & w).]

1b. The Guinness Alice
St James's Gate, Dublin, 1933 pp. 24
[Written by Ronald Barton & Robert Bevan].
Illustrated by John Gilroy
[This Second Edition, coded on last page GA281A, is printed in colour throughout, but has its contents re-arranged and amended as follows: 'A Sane Lunch Party', 'The Walrus and the Carpenter', [Father William], 'Maddening!', 'A Song to Comfort You', '"Off with its Head!" cried the Queen', 'Lobster Quadrille', 'A Head without a Guinness', 'A Tale of Two Glasses', ''Tis the Voice of the Lobster', 'The Hunting of the Stout', 'Second Sight', '"Oh my ears and whiskers!"']

2. The Guinness Legends and Other Verses
Arthur Guinness Son & Co. Ltd, St James's Gate, Dublin, 1934 pp. [24]
[Written by Ronald Barton & Robert Bevan].
Illustrated by John Gilroy

3. Jabberwocky Re-Versed and Other Guinness Versions
St James's Gate, Dublin, 1935 pp. [24]
[Written by Ronald Barton & Robert Bevan].
Illustrated by John Gilroy

4. Songs of Our Grandfathers Re-set in Guinness Time
St James's Gate, Dublin, 1936 pp. [24]
[Written by Ronald Barton, Robert Bevan & Dorothy L. Sayers]. Illustrated by Rex Whistler

5. A Guinness Scrapbook
St James's Gate, Dublin, 1937 10¼in × 8in pp. [24]
[Quotes from literary sources and rhymes by Dorothy L. Sayers and others]. Decorations by Antony Groves-Raines [with additional illustrations by H. M. Bateman, John Gilroy, Rex Whistler, Fougasse, Linley Sambourne & Phiz]

6. Alice Aforethought
Guinness Carrolls for 1938 pp. [20]
[Written by Ronald Barton & Robert Bevan].
Illustrated by Antony Groves-Raines

7. Prodigies and Prodigals
Brought to book by Guinness [1939] pp. [20]
[Written by Ronald Barton & Robert Bevan].
Illustrated by Antony Groves-Raines

(*NOTE:* No further booklets were published until 1950)

8. A Guinness Sportfolio
[1950] pp. [16]
[Written by Stanley Penn & John Trench]. Illustrated by Antony Groves-Raines

9. Album Victorianum
[1951] 10¼in × 8in pp. [16]
[Written by Stanley Penn, John Trench & Ronald Barton. Illustrated by Ronald Ferns, Eric Fraser, Jack Hanna & Bruce Hobbs]

10. Alice Where Art Thou?
More Guinness Carrolling [1952] pp. [12]
[Written by John Trench]. Illustrated by Antony Groves-Raines

11. Untopical Songs
Accompanied by Guinness [1953] pp. [12]
[Written by John Trench]. Illustrated by Ronald Ferns

12. What Will They Think of Next?
A Guinness INVENTory [1954] pp. [12]
[Written by John Trench]. Illustrated by Antony Groves-Raines

13. Game Pie
A Guinness Indoor Sportfolio [1955] pp. [12]
[Written by Stanley Penn & John Trench]. Illustrated by Edward Ardizzone

14. Can This Be Beeton?
A Guinness Gallimaufry [1956] pp. [12]
[Written by John Trench]. Illustrated by Antony Groves-Raines

15. Happy New Lear
[1957] pp. [12]
[Written by Stanley Penn]. Illustrated by John Nash

16. Hobby Horses
With Riders by Guinness [1958] pp. [12]
[Written by Stanley Penn]. Illustrated by Rowland Emett

17. Alice Versary
The Guinness Birthday Book [1959] pp. [12]
[Written by Stanley Penn]. Illustrated by Ronald Ferns

18. Reigning Cats & Dogs
A Guinness Book of Pets [1960] pp. [12]
Verses by Stanley Penn. Illustrated by the late Gerard Hoffnung

19. My Goodness! My Gilbert & Sullivan!
[1961] pp. [12]
Verses by Stanley Penn. Illustrated by Antony Groves-Raines

20. Pen Portraits by A. P. H.
Exhibited by Guinness [1962] pp. [12]
Verses by A. P. Herbert. Illustrated by Michael ffolkes

21. Guinness Nonscience
[1963] pp. [12]
Text by Stanley Penn. Illustrated by Maureen Roffey & Bernard Lodge

22. All My Own Work
The Guinness Do It Yourself Book [1964] pp. [12]
Text by Stanley Penn. Illustrated by John Tribe

23. A Visit to Bedsyde Manor
Guinness's Guide for You [1965] pp. [12]

Text by Stanley Penn. Illustrated by John Vernon Lord

24. A Precsription for Foreing Travel
[1966] pp. [12]
Written by Paul Jennings. Illustrated by John Astrop

INDEX